TREASURE

by

Dana Peters-Colley

For where your treasure is, there will your heart be also.

Matthew 6:21

Treasure

by Dana Peters-Colley

Copyright © 2009, 2008

First Edition, Rev. 1, 2009, First Edition, 2008

www.seaministries.net

ISBN: 978-0-578-03149-1

Printed in the United States of America.

TREASURE

TABLE OF CONTENTS

DEDICATION

This book is dedicated to the forgotten children.

They know who they are.

INTRODUCTION

MY SPRITUAL JOURNEY

In 1999, God got a hold of me in an amazing way. I was a creative manager and production person, who had gotten blown up after 8 ½ years at Disney and was halfway through U.C.L.A.'s screenwriting program, raising two small children, when my husband talked me into a move to Nashville. We thought we were moving to help my husband's music career. We didn't know that God had a bigger plan, a plan to change us and have us receive more of Him.

When we came to Nashville, a songwriter convinced my husband, John Ford Coley, to visit his church. Reluctantly, one Sunday morning in May, we entered the building where we could see that the people all had their hands raised up, worshipping. Not being a church person, I clung tightly to my husband's hand. What was he getting us into? John parked us in a pew that was close to an exit, just in case we needed to bolt and we cautiously entered in. Yet, as we stood in the back, we suddenly felt something in the air, something in our hearts, and it reached in and swept over us like a river, drenching us in a cloud of love. This love was tangible. We, for the first time, experienced the real and powerful presence of God. God was real. He was alive. He was sweeping over us and we both cried that day and for the next eight weeks straight. The power and love of God washed our hearts. It was shocking for us to find out Jesus was so real.

Soon after that, I began having visitations from angels and other open visions. I spent 7 ½ hours a day reading my Bible, as a supernatural unction drove me to receive more and more of the Word. As I ventured further, I began having dreams. Words of knowledge, and signs and wonders became a way of life. For the first six months of the Holy Spirit moving in and willingly taking me over, I heard God in a loud, audible voice talking to me constantly, directing my whole life. Later, His voice got softer, and became that still and small voice.

As I matured, the gifting of prophecy sparked alive inside me, and I was on a quest, a search, to do whatever this God, who covered and drenched me with Holy visitations, words and assistance for others, said to do. I would get so wonderfully covered, intoxicated in His love, that it would just gush out of me like a river and spill onto others.

It's a wonderful journey to follow God like this. God must have known that my heart was right toward Him, that I'd say yes to whatever He wanted, and that it would only get better. I served in the small places, wherever the Lord would lead me. At grocery stores, the Lord would direct me to prophesy over people. At my church, we worked for 3 ½ years volunteering to serve our mid-week dinners. All of this time, the Lord would drop creative projects, books, films in my lap, where I would write and write, create and create, and tuck everything away for the hour of the Lord's release. These things I tried to birth but to no avail. God was teaching me lessons, some of them very hard, and I laid all I had again and again on the altar, for His timing and His uses. As I matured and the years passed, He told me I wouldn't be writing creative projects for awhile and for two more years, I had no desire to write anything. Then, Spiritual book ideas began to pour from heaven, and so that was where I placed my focus along with homeschooling two of my kids.

Then, God told me I was moving into ministry. That week, I was asked to begin serving on a prophetic team under Powerhouse Ministries. After a while, I was leading teams. I was still prophesying anywhere He led, especially at my home church. Sometimes the outpourings of the Holy Spirit were so strong that I would prophesy with great accuracy and precision. It was God in me, either doing the talking and taking over my mouth, or giving me wonderful visions that I would describe and they would minister to people's situations. To serve this way, and have the Lord use me in this way is a wonderful privilege. At one point, the Lord also changed things and I received dreams throughout the night, with interpretations in the morning. God would pour out to me about nations, people, and incidents that were coming. I would intercede and pray, and at times contact people to share what He had shown me. This is the glory. There have been valleys as well, and I have fallen many times but learning, growing and crying out for more of Him.

Recently, the Lord came and gave me my commission and asked me if I would go. My answer, of course, was yes, but I enter this journey not specifically knowing what I will do or how I will go. That's the interesting part of following God. We aren't in charge. He is. Yet, He is trustworthy and good, and loves us so much that He gave His Son to make sure we had a way back to him.

In this book, I will share with you the story of bits and pieces of my journey. I have a tremendously difficult past. My parents divorced when I was 14 in Orange County, California and I was turned loose. I made many, many wrong choices but the one right choice I made was to accept my salvation of Jesus Christ at 14 just before my world came crashing down. I didn't enter a church, except for a short time when a bunch of us lost high schoolers dabbled in it. Yet, Jesus was there, walking with me all that time, and I didn't even know it. I accepted Christ but was unreachable for another decade. Yet, little by little my life improved as I made better and better choices. I went on to college and graduated with honors. I went on to a successful career in entertainment. I married John and I joined a false religion but wasn't very active in it.

My life really, truly changed when we entered a church in Nashville in 1999. The power of God is so real, and it's there but we must be hungry and search until we find it. We can't follow what is comfortable and convenient. We must go after God with all of our hearts. That's what I pray you do with this book! I pray that it helps you to go after God with every fiber of your being because the rewards are endless in their scope, and enlarging in their sphere of where and how you will travel. Remember, God is the ultimate thrill ride and nothing can compete with His greatness!

SPECIAL THANKS

I want to take a moment and thank some people who have made this book possible. First and foremost, my thanks goes to Lord Jesus. He saved me from the pit of hell many times and welcomed me with His grace into loving, safe arms. He is my all and my everything. Second, I want to thank my husband. John Ford Coley, who has been my strength and might supporting my journey. He's my best friend and one I dearly love. Our miles have been long and sometimes hard, but they are well worth what we have achieved in order to take the kingdom for Christ. I want to thank my mom. She found Jesus after many years in the battle. I also want to thank all of my kids. Each one of them is unique and destined for greatness. Lastly, I'd like to thank the following people for their efforts in funding, reading and advising this manuscript: Mishel and Jon Kocheran, Jack Gilbert, Mike Bodayle, Chris Dupre, Bob Anderson, Mike and Marilyn Seth. There are numerous more. Bless you.

TREASURE

CHAPTER ONE

The God of the Universe

spends time thinking about you.

YOU ARE PRECIOUS TREASURE

Did you know that there is no record of pirate treasure maps? None. Yet, this depiction is clearly connected to treasure in our minds. We are looking for the direction, the map, the guidance, to find riches beyond our wildest imaginations. This is what God promises us. God promises us that we will find treasure beyond all we could dream or ask for if we follow Him. He left a map, His words in the Bible. "...Anything that meets the criteria of a "map" describing the location of a "treasure" could appropriately be called a *treasure map.*" [1]

There's a direction, a way we have to go in order to obtain all of the items promised to us. God lays out jewels and treasures right at our feet if we will follow along the path He maps out. First, we must experience God and how He sees us.

YOU ARE TREASURE

I have certain treasures that are valuable to me. They aren't valuable to others. Since God made me special and different from others, and since each one of us is made this way, we need to take a look at what we are treasuring and evaluate if it's really the treasure we want to be. Over the years, I have met

---

[1] Treasure map search: http://en.wikipedia.org/wiki/Treasure_map#Treasure_maps_in_history

many, many people who didn't treasure themselves. I was one of these people in my youth. I didn't feel worthy of being treasure because of family circumstances: sexual abuse, alcoholism, drug abuse. The list goes on and on. In my growing up years there was much that wasn't right. I wasn't treated as valuable and therefore, didn't value myself. That all changed when I encountered the transforming power of Jesus Christ.

God wants you to know YOU ARE TREASURE. You are special treasure to Him. That's why He made you. He made you so He could, as a Papa, see you and enjoy who you are. Think of an adorable little two or three-year old child. If you were that child's parent, you look down and there's your child. She's discovering what sunshine feels like on her face. She's tasting ice cream for the first time. All of what she does brings joy. This is what our Father God feels like. He takes joy in each one of our differences, as well as the ways we are like Him. He is patient with us, just like we would be patient with that two-year old as they are learning and discovered their way. God starts us out on our journey. He unconditionally loves us no matter what we have done. He even loves us in the places that we don't forgive ourselves for what we've done. He sees right down to the core of our hearts and penetrates into places we might have forgotten we had - the good parts. He sees them and wants us to take hold of ourselves and become something great by His values and His standards.

At one point in my life, I didn't feel like treasure. I had left a troubled, drug infested marriage, moved in with my mom and through bad choices, her husband made me homeless. He was a troubled man, a veteran who was disabled. World War II had taken its toll on his well-being when he watched his fellow sailors eaten by sharks in the Pacific. Mom's husband suddenly had a young woman in his house with her two-year old child, and she was dabbling in a strange religion. These demonic prayers I was saying added to my step-father's mental state which became dangerous. I had a psychiatrist call me and tell me my life was in danger and I needed to move out right away. Needless to say, I did move out but had no place to go.

I had some money but no one would rent to me. I was a full time student with no job. At this point, John Ford Coley was my friend and allowed me to stay at a house that was above his apartment. The owners were on vacation in Europe. Here I was twenty-five years old, a single parent, having left a husband who wasn't able to quit drugs, and a full time college student, completely abandoned. No one believed in me enough to rent to me, and I had no family I could count on. It was a petrifying experience. I did not feel like I was treasure. I felt like every right move I made ended up in disaster.

So, I stayed at the house but slept on the floor because I didn't feel good enough to sleep in their beds. I didn't even know if these people knew I was in their home. After about a week of looking and looking for an apartment, I finally relaxed. I just decided that I would enjoy life and go to the beach instead of hunt for an apartment. At that point, I let go, which was what God was waiting for. When I let go, it gave God room to come into my situation.

You may be wondering why I would be calling on God, being in this strange religion and all. However, I did know Him. When I was 14 years old, I took Christ on a teen hotline and He had been walking with me ever since. When I joined this false religion, my one statement was that I could not deny Christ – and they said, "You won't have to." So, I took Jesus with me right into that wrong religion because I didn't have enough of Jesus in me to know what was Him and what wasn't.

God knows His own. He knows which ones are going to be His. I was calling to Him when I was calling out to the wrong god. He knows everything and knew the plan He ultimately had for me. He was just watching His treasure have a melt down. One thing about treasure, if it's boiling and being melted completely down, that's not the time to touch it. After it cools down a bit, but while it is still pliable, that's when you can put your hands on it and mold it into the shape you want it to become. That's what God did with me. I relaxed and He touched the situation. God will let us come to the end of ourselves in order to find Him. One thing about God, He is not afraid of things getting hot. Difficult situations allow God to come into our situations and become bigger.

The day that I went to the beach, in the late afternoon, John and I drove around and found an apartment. The owners were inside painting and John did his wonderful best at meeting them. I got the apartment and my Mom joined me. That day I learned a valuable lesson that I have had to repeatedly learn again and again. No matter what happened, God was taking care of me. It sure didn't look the way I wanted it to look. It didn't happen the way it should have happened. Yet, God was right there, providing shelter, and eventually a place to live. I was being melted down to the end of me, to the worst God knew I could handle, so that He could show me what I was made of – what the God of heaven had made me out of – and it was strong stuff. There were many more bad decisions that I would make but God was right there to help show me the way along my "treasure map" in life, and lead me through.

Are you lost in your way? Did you know that God is right there with you, alongside, walking with you? If you haven't taken Christ, here's your chance. If you want to become treasure, God's personal treasure, take this moment to tell

Jesus,
I have made mistakes and I need your forgiveness.
Please save me.
Please come into my heart and change me.
I give my life to you, knowing that you died for me.
I take you as my Lord and Savior.
Amen.

God you are sorry for what you have done, ask Jesus Christ into your heart, and God will begin walking and talking to you.

Another thing that God does when He treasures you is that He sends people to help you. He sent John to be there as I went, the people who owned the house I stayed at, the apartment owners who just happened to be painting that day, and my mother, who joined my side and was there as I struggled to finish college. Always be on the lookout for who God will send to help you. They are angels in your path.

This walk we take through life is how God develops us to become treasure. He takes us through situations and then, we are tested. He repeats the process again and again, throughout our lives as we develop into becoming greater and greater treasure. As I borrowed that house, and slept on the floor, I didn't feel like treasure. I felt worthless and unusable, and being punished for what I thought I was doing that were the right things in life. Yet, God knew what He was doing. He knew just the tests, just the circumstances, just the situations that would lead me to Him.

Do you feel like treasure? Do you feel like you are special and have been made for a purpose that drives you on the inside? If you feel like you are treasure, then, this book will help you to go even further. If you don't feel like you are treasure, this book will help you get in touch with what you treasure, how you are God's treasure, and what is valuable to God.

> We are God's treasure!
>
> Now therefore,
> If you will indeed
> obey My Voice
> and keep
> My Covenant
> then you shall be
> a special treasure
> to Me above all people;
> for all the earth is
> Mine.
>
> Exodus 19:5
> NKJV

Let's remember a few things. Number One: we are made in God's image and we are precious treasure to God.

Treasure here (Strong's Concordance - Hebrew 5459) means: wealth, as closely shut up, jewel, peculiar treasure, proper, good, special. It's the same meaning for treasure when in Scripture God says: For the Lord hath chosen Jacob unto Himself, and Israel for His peculiar treasure. We will get to the story of Jacob in a bit.

Definition of treasure:

Wesbster's Dictionary Definition

treasure:

1) wealth (as money, jewels or precious metals) stored up or hoarded

2) riches

3) a store of money in reserve

4) something of great worth or value

5) also, a person esteemed as rare or precious

Now that we have discovered that we <u>are</u> treasure, let's look at *what* we treasure.

What do you treasure?

• TIME

Do you treasure time? The way to determine this is how willing are you to give away your time? How much of your time will you give to things you might never get anything back for in return? How much time do you waste in a day? If time is precious to you, you might value how much of it you will share with others. Think of time as gold, gold in your hands. How do you spend your gold? Do you just throw it away? Do you think about it much?

• POSSESSIONS

How many things do you have? How many things do you have to take care of? If Jesus were sitting in the room, what would He say about your stuff? Do you easily give things away? Do you give away your best things or do you give away things that are broken? How many things do you have and how long have you had your things? What are you holding onto that might be good for you to let go of? Do you trust God to give you more things? Do you hold onto your things like you hold onto memories? Or are you afraid that the past is better than the future God has for you? Maybe possessions, your things are your treasure.

• RELATIONSHIPS

How much time do you spend with God? Is He a Sunday guy to you, or a guy you have just met? Do you spend much time with your family and friends? Do you stay longer at work just to hear a friend's side of the story? Do you talk behind your friend's backs when no one is looking? How do you value relationships and do you treat them as you want to be treated? Are relationships a treasure to you?

• POWER

Are you happy with where you are in life? Do you get seated at the best seats when you go to a concert, a party, or church gathering? Do you relax when you are driving in traffic or do you panic and have to get out of line to get ahead of the cars in front of you? Have you been promoted in your job recently? Do those around you value you? How you answer these questions can help you decide how you feel about power. It's not just the outward power that comes from being king of the hill, it's the little things that make up how you treasure yourself in life and where you fit in the mix of life with others.

• PRIVACY

Do you like your alone time? Do you value yourself as an individual to spend time with no one else but you for a day, a week, a month? When you are in a group would you describe yourself as trusting, or safe, or transparent? Do you think anyone really knows you - the good, the bad, and the ugly? How you feel about your private, intimate self with others tells a lot about if you treasure privacy.

• SUCCESS

Many people have success but their definitions of success are different. For some people, just getting out of bed in the morning is success. For others, it's the achievement of their dreams on their terms. In order to determine if success is your treasure, you could determine how you feel about yourself in the grand scheme of things, what goals you set for yourself and if you are achieving that end. For some, it's greatly important. For others, their focus is not on it and therefore, they don't accomplish much because they set no goals. Is success something you treasure?

• TRAVEL

Some people value where they are going and where they have been. They dream of a trip to Europe, a mission to Africa, a day at the beach. It might even be a fishing trip to the lake. Do you value going and being somewhere else than where you are? Do you think about foreign nations? Do you consider taking up other languages and do you romanticize about what it will be like when you get there? Then, travel might be something you treasure.

• FAMILY

I have met women who told me that they never considered having children, it just wasn't in what they considered for their lives. I have met others who want large families that will take nations for God. Inside each person, there is a dream, a hope planted and a desire to fulfill it. With some, it comes at great cost, losing child after child until they meet success. Others yearn to adopt. Some people make friends their family. Others would rather go it alone. Do you treasure family?

These categories have given you an opportunity to think about what you individually treasure and what is important to you. Treasure has a far broader meaning when we investigate it. It's much bigger than diamonds and rubies. It's broader than houseboats and maid service. Treasure adds life to life. It adds value. It makes the journey worth it. Now, let's move into seeing what God thinks about treasure. I hope that I will inspire you to receive how God sees you so that you can realize your potential as His Treasure.

At the beginning of this chapter, you learned that there were no real treasure maps. Yet, in the first book of the Bible, Genesis, God describes a treasure when He builds the earth. It is surrounded by four rivers and called Eden. Everything that was ever needed was there for Adam and then, God added the woman to befriend and walk with Adam. To add the best part, the Creator of the Universe came and walked with him in the cool of the day. So, Adam was given the ultimate friend who wanted to spend time with him. There was even gold in one of the rivers, so every treasure was available for Adam and Eve, and best of all, God came and walked with Adam in the cool of the day.

Adam, as most everyone knows, was evicted from the Garden. He and Eve had done the one thing God had required of them not to do and the map was removed for entry into the garden. Yet, God still wanted to walk with men. When He was betrayed, He still yearned to have relationship with what was made in His image. Even when we behave like a worm, God loves us.

Now, let's look at Jacob, a descendent of Adam, and the second son of Isaac. Jacob was born with a promise over his life. Yet, his name means "heel grabber," which is what he did to his twin brother Esau when they came into the world. Esau wasn't too intelligent but he was his father's favorite. Jacob, on the other hand, was his mother's favorite. Esau came in one day and wanted a bowl of soup. For the soup, he gave up his right to having all the treasure of what it meant to be the older brother to Jacob. He probably thought it was all a joke but God didn't see it that way. Then, many years later, as Isaac lay close to death, he wanted to bless his son and Jacob's mom, Rebecca, had Jacob go in wearing a hairy arm piece so he felt like his brother and get the blessing. It was a deceitful thing to do but Jacob went along with it. Jacob got the blessing and Esau didn't.

That's the back story. You now have the setup for Jacob's situation. Jacob is a worm. He is willing to sell out his brother and even pose as his brother to get what he wants. Yet, in many later generations, God consistently refers to the blessing that is on Jacob. God still loved Jacob. God loves us right in our mess because He is working out a plan, a story, a triumph, an amazing tale with each one of our lives. God now has a hero who doesn't seem like a hero. Jacob, the worm, he's our hero. He represents the worst in all of us, and God is showing us we can have pasts, be full of all sorts of selfish ways – and God still loves us. So, what does God add to the situation? God does two things.

FIRST IN JACOB'S JOURNEY: A GOD ENCOUNTER

Jacob ran from his brother who had vowed to kill him. Think of some very hairy man, who likes to hunt, chasing after you to kill you. So, Rebecca, Jacob's mom sent him to her brother's house. When we are treasure, we are often driven into desperate situations to take us into our destiny. On the path from our bad situation God will show up, and that's just what He did.

Jacob slept upon a rock along the way. Jacob fell asleep and God showed up. Jacob dreamt a dream where angels ascended and descended from heaven.

Once you have had a God encounter, things are forever different. You experience realities that have greater truth than what is right here in front of you in the natural and they forever change the way you view everything. God met Jacob in his dilemma and this encounter changed Jacob from behaving like a worm, into becoming a man of great destiny. One God encounter will do that to you.

Have you had a God encounter? Have you experienced God or have you found Him distant? He doesn't want to be distant. As I stated, when God created Adam, He wanted to walk with him in the cool of the day.[2] God wants to have a relationship with us but it's up to us to seek Him out. We need to get enough of God in us to know His ways. That comes from reading our Bibles, and hearing enough Word of God that we can begin that transformation process. Jacob was the grandson of Abraham. He was part of God's kingdom, in the Church as you would say. He was under the promise, so as he ran for his life, having sinned, he was met by God.

For me, I had accepted Jesus as my Savior but my real God encounter came when I entered a Spirit-filled church and felt the Presence of God. God is meant to be experienced.

As Jacob journeyed, God opened up heaven and Jacob experienced it. That's why he called the place Bethel, House of God. Before this, it was called Luz. It was a place of trees. At the root, this word means to depart or be perverse. God loves to work in parables, which are little stories that teach you the same meaning, or metaphors, which establish true meanings for us. God is a good teacher. Here, in Luz, he took the place and it was the place where you should depart from and turned it into the House of God – where the gate of heaven opened and ladders appeared with angels going down and going back up. God took a man who was like a worm and met him in a perverse place he

---

[2] Genesis 3:8

should depart from, and in God's love, God opened up heaven and changed the man. This is a metaphor for every one of us that comes to God. We are like Jacob. When Christ changes us, who we are and where we are changes entirely when we have a Jesus encounter. Yet, we have an even greater covenant because God doesn't just come and show us heaven, He actually puts heaven inside of us.

Like Jacob, we are destined to be treasure. God is the one holding the treasure map and we only can see the end picture that God shows us of what our possibilities are, and step out into what we don't know and the Lord directs our steps.[3]

Let's look again at the concept of treasure hunting. What does it entail? Here are five things hunting for treasure promises us:

1) risk of death
2) leaving behind comfort – what is normal and safe
3) doing things exactly by the rules
4) promise of adventure
5) promise of amazing riches

This is just what following Christ promises us.

FIRST: RISK OF DEATH

As we follow, Jesus warns us that we may have to give up our physical lives and not deny Him. Many are doing this around the world and we must not forget that this is the price of admission into the kingdom of God. It may be asked of us and we need to be prepared for it. Yet, one true God encounter will make it impossible for us to deny the one who has saved our lives because we taste of a kingdom more real than what we experience here on earth. Kingdom

---

[3] Proverbs 16:9

reality is a greater reality than our earthly reality because it sticks with us, it absorbs us and we can draw from its memory because it is everlasting.

Our risk of death also occurs as we lay down our old life and pick up our new life in Christ. We are birthed into a new life in God's kingdom and that is the born-again experience. Yet, we must also die to our old nature. Remember, the wages of sin is death but the gift of God is eternal life through Jesus Christ our Lord.[4] So, our God reaches across the universe and for what we have done wrong, He offers us a never-ending life with Him. How much of that life we receive is up to us. We need to go after God as we receive salvation. Remember though, God set a pattern in motion. Whatever we give up to God, comes back to us much greater.[5] He is that good.

SECOND: LEAVING BEHIND COMFORT

Our second point in treasure hunting is that we begin to leave behind what is comfortable and do the impossible. We shift and change as God changes us, and we throw out the values that are not God's and we adopt His. These ways that we may have to walk might not be easy for us, and they might not be comfortable and convenient. God may begin to stretch us out of this old way we thought and behaved. Then, we must go the distance in order to receive the prize.

Before I discovered and began the real walk in Christ, I was a pro-choice, woman libber, don't-tell-me-what-to-do kind of woman. Then, as He gently began to change things, I began to see the world from His perspective and one-by-one my values shifted. The only thing that I wanted was to make Him happy and that meant that I had come out from the way I thought the world existed and receive a world from heaven. These values always have the foundation of love at their core, rather than judgment. Yet, they stand against what may be

---

[4] Romans 6:23

[5] Matthew 19:29

considered convenient in our culture or politically correct. We have to stand up to what is going on around us, even if that is not comfortable. One of my most favorite verses in the Bible is John 3:17. Jesus says, "For God sent not his Son into the world to condemn the world; but that the world through Him might be saved."

As we move out of what might feel convenient, and speak up, and stand up for what is right, and do what the Lord would do, we gain access to more of the kingdom because we are moving by our actions. Standing up for what is right and learning how to do this in love, not losing our peace in the process, is something we develop over time as we experience more and more of the kingdom. The key is making sure we're abiding in Christ. When we come out into our flesh, into our anger, our frustration, fear and control then, we lose the ground we are working to gain. However, it is the process we must all go through as we grow as believers. Jesus tells us we'll know believers by their fruit. A good man brings forth good. An evil man brings forth evil.[6] We must do what isn't convenient to further the kingdom, cry out to Christ as we make mistakes to help us, and stick with it and not give up on ourselves when we stumble but pick up and keep going so we can experience even greater levels that God has for us.

THIRD: THE RULES

This takes us to the third point: The rules. We people like rules. We like to live inside more and more of them, until we burst. There are some of us that like the rules just so we can break them. None of us can keep the rules. We can get really bound up in this and God knows it. God made it so that we operate above the rules, and He writes the rules on our hearts.[7] God is above the law and Jesus is coming from heaven with heavenly laws that supersede earthly laws.

---

[6] Luke 6:43-45

[7] Hebrews 8:10-12

When I refer to law here, I am saying that God doesn't do things legalistically but through the greatest law of love. He does not get bound up.

God uses the struggle against doing things the "world's way" or a way where we as people will put God inside of a box where they feel some level of control, to having to let go of control in order to follow God. If we truly follow God, we must take the rules, and have a level of reverence for them, but also see that God may lead us in ways that will not make sense to our minds in order to work out His plan.

Following God is crazy to the rational mind. Abraham, the father of the Jewish nation was told by God, "Follow me."

"Where are we going, God?"

No answer.

Follow me is the direction. Abraham knows it is God. He just follows.

As we follow in ways that may seem strange to the world's way of doing things, we experience God in ways we thought were impossible. God gets bigger and the ways of the world, the ways of the world's "rules" of what you should have, what you should "do" get left behind. We see how God is over and above our situations which work out even when they shouldn't. God shows up with signs and wonders following. He does the impossible because He's God. It gives Him joy to see our amazement of Him.

Remember, it's faith that pleases God. We don't disregard the rules of God's Word but we also walk by this faith and we are right in our churches. We have covering over us to make sure we're protected. We are doing the things God wants us to do in our homes, places of work, in our families. God created the rules knowing we'd fall short, but it shows us how much we need a Savior, like Jesus, who is so compassionate and full of love that He would break the rules of His time, like observing the Sabbath, which is a day of no work in the

Old Testament, by healing one woman who was sick for eighteen years.[8] Did God want us to take a day and rest? You bet. However, there are times where we lay down the rule and apply the greater law, which is love, and on our day of rest go and help the one in need.

FOURTH: PROMISE OF ADVENTURE

Our fourth point is where it gets exciting. God shows up with signs and wonders as we follow Him. Amazing revelations and doors open to us. Mysteries unfold that are beyond belief. Miracles happen. God makes the journey so amazing that we can't go back. He's having things happen that wouldn't normally occur. He has things show up in our lives. People know things and tell them to us and we're amazed because they had no way of knowing. Things line up in ways we could never have guessed. He fills us with a peace we can't begin to describe at times that we would have acted in such a different way. There's no going back. We are wrecked for the world because we have tasted heaven. If we are believers, this is our right. We're told that we might have life and life more abundantly. Many aren't receiving this life in the body but all have the possibility of receiving life and life more abundantly.

God put adventure into the formula when He created us. Look at the Bible. It's full of what has occurred in adventure. There are Queens like Esther who save their nations. There are mighty men like David who slay Goliaths. There are donkeys that talk. There are rainbows as signs. There are miracles of people getting healed. If you aren't experiencing this journey as the most exciting adventure you ever imagined, then, you're either being prepared, or you're not crying out for more from your Maker. He made heaven and earth. He made everything. So, cry out and ask Him to give you the adventure. Ask him to show you if anything has blocked you from entering into all He's got for you and get on board! If you want the adventure, though, you must be willing to pay the

---

[8] Luke 13:11-16

price to get it. It might cost you everything. However, remember, whatever you give He gives you much, much more in return. This is the promise of what it is to be 'in Christ'. If you're a believer, you have the right to this promise.

FIFTH: PROMISE OF RICHES

Riches can be earthly and there was gold in one of the rivers that came to Eden, but more valuable riches are those that are heavenly. We can't get saved by anything we've done. In fact, the worse off we are the better because the angels rejoice at the salvation of one sinner who comes to God more than 99 good people,[9] and Jesus described that those that have sinned much love much.[10] You realize how terrible it is out there and how great it is with Him. You don't take Him for granted because you remember what it was like to not have Him. He becomes your riches. He gives you earthly things but He comes inside of you and there is a richness of life you experience that you wouldn't give up for anything. This abundant life is what you were created to experience.

If you haven't experienced enough of this, let's say a prayer and get you into more! Please say this aloud. There's power in your voice:

God,
I want all you have and more!
Will you please give me a God encounter, Lord?
Show me anything that will block me here
so that I can have all that you have for me!
I want to be on the amazing journey,
so I am asking for this. In Jesus Name, Amen.

[9] Luke 15:7

[10] Luke 7:47

Now, let's get back to Jacob. After he has this God encounter his approach changes. He would have figured out some shifty way to change things by his own underhanded efforts, but he comes under his situation and sticks with it.

Remember, I stated there were two things that God did for Jacob. The first thing that happened with Jacob was the God encounter. The second unfolded when he got to uncle Laban's house.

SECOND IN JACOB'S JOURNEY : HE DISCOVERS LOVE

The second thing God did was send "love"! Jacob, who fled from his enemy, poor betrayed brother Esau, went to uncle Laban's. Maybe the reason why Jacob's mother liked Jacob so much was that he reminded her of her own brother, Laban. There, Jacob sees Rachel. He falls head over heels in love with her. He wants her so much he can't think straight and for seven long years he pines away for her and works hard to obtain the right to marry her.

Let's remember, Jacob did a deceitful thing in his family. He did a set up on his brother and so, it came back and bit him. This is key. Even if we have had a God encounter, if we have committed an act that goes against God, unless God supernaturally intervenes we are still going to have to pay for it. What Jacob did to Esau caused Laban, on the night of Jacob's marriage to do a similar thing to him. Laban sent Jacob his older daughter, who had bad eyesight, Leah. It must have been a great wedding feast that night because Jacob didn't know it wasn't Rachel until the morning. What he had done to Esau was now done to him. A bait and switch.

First bait and switch: Esau was called by his father, but Jacob's mother sent him instead. Second bait and switch: Laban gave Rachel to Jacob, but sent Leah instead.

The principles of sowing and reaping are evident here. There is a passage that God has used with me for the longest time when He speaks to me and only recently did I look up this Scripture. God, in my prayer time when He talks to me, would say these words. God is not mocked. I finally looked up the meaning of this Scripture. It's Galatians 6:7-8. "Be not deceived; God is not mocked: for whatsoever a man soweth, that shall he also reap. For he that soweth to the flesh reap corruption; but he that soweth to the Spirit shall of the Spirit reap life everlasting."

By sowing, or planting an act of deceit, Jacob received it back and it cost him seven years, and possibly seven more. He might have walked right into favor instead of labor had he been listening to God. Still, God had a plan for his life and God was merciful to give him an encounter so that his life would be transformed. God sees everything. That is the meaning of 'God is not mocked'. We can't get anything by Him. He sees us, every part and piece of our heart, saved or unsaved, lost or found. Every action, thought, detail, it all is seen by God. What we do is going to have a result. God is always watching and the good news is while He is watching, He wants to love us. Yet, He may have to break us to make us.

This is an Old Testament account. As Christians who are under the New Covenant, which is the better covenant[11] we can ask forgiveness and through the blood of Jesus can receive grace and mercy from Christ who intercedes for us. Yet, we will still go through trials and testing. God knows best how to grow us into places of maturity – and why would He do that? So that we can have more! God wanted to give Jacob more. He wants to give you more!

Back to our Scripture account. If Jacob had done things God's way rather than his mother's way, he might have saved himself seven years of hard labor. Still, love triumphed and Jacob got Rachel. He also married Leah whom God

---

[11] Hebrews 8:6

also loved. Jacob received 12 sons, who became the 12 tribes of Israel. Jacob left a mighty legacy. God had done what was needed to mature Jacob with one God encounter so that he submitted under his uncle Laban instead of twisting out of the deal because he had experienced something in God's kingdom that changed the way he did things.

We have learned two things here. God loves us and helps us, even when we are worms![12] We are all worms, saved or unsaved, because we all fall short and sin. Yet, God is right there to help us with things. As it was told to me, the coal in Jacob's life was turned into a diamond. God comes down to meet us in encounters that are priceless. He grows us and once we accept Jesus as Lord and Savior, He never leaves us nor forsakes us[13]. God sends love into our lives so that we discover that we are precious treasure.

This love affair God had with Jacob is the same one He wants with you. Are you willing to lay down what you treasure to receive the treasure God wants to give to you?

Will you lay down what you treasure?

- your time?

- your possessions?

- your relationships?

- your power?

- your privacy?

- your success?

- your travel?

- your family?

---

[12] Isaiah 41:14

[13] Hebrews 13:5

Jesus did this for us. He obtained the treasure of the whole world for following the treasure map that God led him to follow. He was hunting for treasure and it required: 1) the risk of death; 2) his leaving behind comfort of what was normal and safe; 3) his not doing things by a religious 'legalistic' rule system; 4) the promise of adventure; and 5) the promise of amazing riches.

Jesus is hunting for treasure and that treasure is you.

YOU ARE PRECIOUS TREASURE

Will you accept the journey, the adventure God has ahead? Have you begun the journey but let fear hold you back? Whatever you are feeling about yourself – just say yes to Christ so that you can have all God wants to give you. You are precious treasure that God created and is moving into great destiny, plan, and purpose. Keep going my friend, He has so much in store for you.

Now, let's move to the next chapter where we will discover how we can leave what is dead behind.

TREASURE

CHAPTER TWO

EGYPTIANS and TREASURES OF OLD

Sometimes we hold onto things

God wants us to let go of.

LEAVE THE DEAD BEHIND

Like a disintegrating, crumbling ship at the bottom of the ocean, the things that are decaying in our lives are difficult at best for us to look at. Yet, they are still things that are dead. If we try to hold on to what is dead, we are taken down under, where there is no breath for us to be what God wants us to be.

Have you ever seen something with no life in it? Facing the death in our lives can be a bit disarming. The ancient Egyptians must have thought so, for they developed all sorts of ways to keep from facing extinction when they physically died. The Kings of Egypt made their reservations and took their families, servants and even pets, building all sorts of things to take with them. They thought they needed their bodies and all of their stuff in the place that they were going. What a great big surprise they must have discovered when they reached the other side of life and found out that their formula for dealing with death didn't work.

Many people do this with God. They play games with their minds, believing this false way or that, whatever feels "right" at the time. They take their whole future and don't seek the one and true God and their misguided realities are like those ancient Egyptians, they will wind up with the wrong answers. In the life and death aspect of things, Jesus was crystal clear when He said, "...I am the way, the truth, and the life. No one comes to the Father except through Me." [14]

The only way to heaven is through Jesus Christ. It hasn't changed. It might not be nice or politically correct, but these are the words of Jesus Christ and therefore, we must take it by faith. Otherwise, we can easily wind up like those ancient Egyptians. We have made all sorts of plans, but when we get to the other side we are in for quite a surprise. If you are not a Christian and want to receive some sort of conformation, then ask God to show you who He is. Ask Jesus to show you that he is real. Cry out for this and watch what He does. You see, God isn't afraid of who He is...are you?

I was completely amazed to find out that not only was God real, but He wanted to come inside of me, take all of the junk out of me, and transform me into His likeness. What I received for the so-called death that occurred in my old life was a new life with so much more joy and supernatural experiences happening that often, it feels like I am living out an action-adventure movie because amazement and wonder happen daily.

However, I am getting ahead of what we are here in this chapter to conquer. We are here to conquer death. You see, this is just what Jesus Christ did for us. He went to the grave and three days later He came up, and conquered death. This is why there is so much power in Jesus Christ's blood. That's what God has the ability to do. God has the ability to conquer death in our physical lives, as well as anything that represents death to us. Anything that creates separation from God is dead. These are areas in our lives that are not surrendered to God caused by sin, wrong belief systems, or by generational curses. In this chapter, we will go through some of these areas of death so that we can get rid of this and move into becoming the treasure that God wants us to be.

---

[14] John 14:6 NIV

As we follow Christ, we have to leave the dead behind. If we are a new believer, we must pour ourselves into this process of becoming this new creation by discovering what God's Word says about what we believe, and even if we don't understand it yet, we must ask God to reveal His truth to us. When we receive our salvation and have the born-again experience, we must lay down our own worldly realities and follow God's leading to discover the kingdom's realities. If we have been a believer for some time, we must make sure we stay surrendered to what God is doing because a lot of the time what He does doesn't make sense to us. If we have been saved a long time and have a lot of Word in us, we must ask God to continue to refresh us and keep us where we are becoming more and more Christ-like in our ways. This growth process doesn't stop just because we have been believers for a while. It's a continuous process of growth.

As new believers are added to our church bodies, we must make sure we're not like the prodigal brother and allow ourselves to become offended because of what we see happening, but we must embrace the lost with all of our hearts, realizing that God has gone out and found that one lost sheep and wants us to help bring that person into the kingdom that we have had the joy of being in. At each level, there is a human being who needs to leave behind their old ways, their sin and come into more of what is God.

Here's a description of what we have to do. God is the same yesterday, today and forever.[15] Yet, God is always doing a new thing. So, as we follow God we must realize that we have to leave what might have worked yesterday behind. God continually moves into new seasons, new ways, and we must anchor ourselves inside of Him and Him alone.

Let me illustrate this by telling the story of a ship.

---

[15] Hebrews 13:8

At the bottom of the Sea of Galilee, an ancient ship was discovered.[16] Some believe it was the boat that Jesus was in when he commanded the sea to be still.[17] This 2,000 year-old relic was so deteriorated and delicate that it had to stay underwater for years and years as the preservation process was completed. The boat can show us how we as human beings respond to the reality of God. Here, this item came from a tree that was once alive. It was created so that God could use it to show us that in our storms, we can be calm. He was saying to us, why are you worrying? I have a plan for you and you can trust me, even when there are storms that arise in your life. The thing – the boat – had a time of its use and then, it was dead. The boat sank to the bottom of the Sea of Galilee where it lay for 2,000 years.

I personally think it is terrific that the people have worked to resurrect this dead boat and preserve it, teaching us the average size and what this kind of boat it is. However, what if we made the boat the center of our belief system? What if we built our whole theology on this one verse, and this one historical artifact? Then, we would be out of balance. We would be focused on the dead rather than being led by progressive revelation, and the entirety of the Word of God in the Bible.

The point: God is continually working on each one of us and we only arrive when Jesus comes in all His glory and transforms us completely. We cannot become set in our position, our ways, or our lives, but if we are to remain full of life, we must be continually green. Green things that grow need good soil, water, and fresh sunshine in order to grow. The boat, made from a tree, had become petrified at the bottom of the sea. At some point it was alive but it died when it stopped moving forward, when it could no longer hold water and do what it was designed to do.

---

[16] www.leaderu.com/theology/craftmatches.html. Jerusalem Christian Review © 1998.

[17] Mark 4:39

We must leave the dead behind and always be ready for what God is going to do next. If we are new believers, we must leave behind that old life we had back there and embrace the new one we have in Christ. If we've walked with Christ a long time, we must be ready to embrace the next move of God in our experience of him and never believe that just because we've been walking with him a long time, we aren't going to experience new things. God is always about doing new things.

DEAD MEN TELL NO TALES

My favorite words from anything Disney is 'Dead men tell no tales' inside the Pirates of the Caribbean ride at Disneyland. It comes just before you take your first drop into the darkness. This phrase couldn't be further from the truth for us who follow Christ. As we believers drop into darkness, our experience is of being in the world, but not of the world.[18] We see dead men everywhere. There are dead men walking all over the planet and they tell all sorts of tales. Yet, what they are saying is man's truth and not God's truth. If you don't have Jesus Christ, you are dead. I have literally seen gray coverings on people who do not have their salvation and are operating in a level of sin. They live inside of a death that covers them and they don't even know it. Since words are containers for power and if their containers have life in them, they will attract the life that is in God. If their words, which as I stated are containers for power attract death, they will cause the man to stumble and fall into some pretty deep pits. Anything that goes contrary to the Word is death.

The precious gift of salvation is only our first step toward discovering the amazing abundance of the kingdom of life. We must seize life with everything we have and that is how we must approach Scripture. As we eat our Word, and listen to the Word, we become alive with it. The Word of God has life-giving

---

[18] John 17:13-26

power inside of it that we don't even realize is there and it grows inside of us, changing our character from the inside out.

Let's go on so that I can make some points about what life and death mean in the kingdom of God. Let's remember two important points that are our foundation of why we want to get rid of what is dead in our lives. Scripture says:

1) Death and life are in the power of the tongue.[19]

2) My people are destroyed for a lack of knowledge.[20]

I remember when as a new believer, God inspired me to study the Word 7 1/2 hours a day. It was an amazing holy unction and I now know it wasn't just for me, it was for where I was going (and at the age of 40 I was also making up for all those lost years not reading the Word!). At that time, I came across Deuteronomy 28. This verse in the Bible opened up huge doors for me to understand a world that did not make sense to me. Here we live in the world where there is destruction, there is starvation, there are awful, awful things going on. Then, there are wonderful things going on as well. Deuteronomy 28 teaches us about blessings and cursings. There are 1,000 generations of blessings that come down on those who have good, Godly people in their generational lines.[21] There are up to four generations of curses for those who hate God.[22] However, with each new generation, there can be more curses to perpetuate some pretty serious stuff.

This Scripture allowed me to see life and death at the higher level of how it affected the entire world. Now, I understood why some people were more blessed, and others were more cursed. They need Jesus. They need the transforming experience that the Holy Spirit brings in order to change their cities, nations and the future generations.

[19] Proverbs 18:21

[20] Hosea 4:6

[21] Deuteronomy 7:9

[22] Exodus 20:5

When I was in college, I minored in political science focusing on international relations. I had one graduate course that dealt with political violence, studying places that had more tribulation versus places where there was more peace. The one analysis that arose from the course was the belief that places where there was democracy, you received stabilized nations. I believe that democracy was not the answer. I believe the Christian foundation is the answer. If the principles in Scripture are embraced by a culture, which are the fundamental principles of treating each other with a level of dignity, then, the foundational basic human rights are respected. Order that comes from those that respect their governments and each other, who behave in Godly love, and this will automatically bring order. Therefore, whole families will raised in balance and the outcome is a society established that embraces goodness.

This is what Jesus Christ does to us. We receive Him in our hearts and His love gives us the love for our brothers and sisters, the lost, the broken-hearted, and the suffering. God fills inside of us and our selfish ways, and the way that is dead is replaced with what comes down from heaven. Jesus truly is the answer to all of our problems! It is only the love of God, the mercy of God, who sends his only Son Jesus to take this from us. Jesus took all of this sin at Calvary and as we come to follow Jesus, there is a removal of this sin. We sincerely say we're sorry and then, it's gone. Jesus brings a new and better covenant.[23]

In dealing with getting rid of what is dead in us, as the body of Christ, there are two ways that I see believers operate. There are those who have been raised with generational blessings that come with following the Lord. Then, there are those who have gone through great trials and tribulations in order to come inside the kingdom. Each one has a set of tests coming from opposite directions. The lost must come into the kingdom and allow the love of God to pour over all of their wounds for what they have suffered. They must allow

---

[23] Hebrews 10:16-18

themselves the healing process that God is providing them. They suffer much attack inside the body of Christ from well-intentioned believers, but these believers have not experienced the war that the lost have been through just to make it inside the blessed doors of salvation.

The tests for believers, who have lived a blessed life, for they have come easily toward the kingdom and operated inside of it, is to remember to be Christ to the body. They·must not get proud in their own blessing but must pour themselves out like the Lord, to help others and grow in compassion, clothing the naked, healing the sick. God referred to this lack of love in believers when He called them His "stiff necked people"[24] and we as the body of Christ must keep ourselves in check not to allow our blessings to become an area of pride for us. Once we are living in the kingdom with all its wonder, joy and blessings, we must remember not be like those who had the law but forgot the love.

If you find yourself in the camp of difficulty as you follow Christ, there are two good results from what you have gone through. God has allowed these things in your life to give you a bigger reach, a bigger use for Him in the kingdom. Do whatever you can to get freedom. Be open to receive the many wonderful ministries that God has set in place to help you. Cry out to the Lord for help. He hears you. Once you go through these things, you can help others go through them, too.

No matter what direction we are going in as the body of Christ, we are all developing in the fruits of the Spirit. The fruits are love, joy, peace, longsuffering, gentleness, goodness, faith, meekness, temperance (or self control): against such there is no law. [25] If we don't have enough of the fruits of these characteristics, then we are not witnesses to the world for Christ. Let's look at what would be the opposite of these characteristics to see what areas we

---

[24] Exodus 33:3, Acts 7:51

[25] Galatians 5:22

might need to be working on. If we have any and this means any area of the following: hatred, lack of peace, anger, areas that cause us to have a short temper, harshness, evil, no belief, and can't control ourselves, then we are still working on developing our fruit. It's a good thing that Scripture says that the Lord is not slack concerning His promise, as some men count slackness, but is long-suffering to us-ward, not willing that any should perish, but that all should come to repentance.[26] It just proves to us that we are always in need of a Savior and for us to remember to work out our salvation with fear and trembling.[27] When we are dead in areas, God cannot shine through. Jesus Christ died, was raised from the dead and is seated next to God, sending the Holy Spirit to guide us into more of Him so that we can take this planet for the kingdom. We don't want to be dead in any area of our lives.

Our lives need to be a testimony to the world so that we can help our Lord take more territory. Let me illustrate this in a story, to get you thinking about what can bring death in our lives from not following what the Word of God says. There was a family who considered themselves Christians. There were parents and a son. The son attended parochial school. The parents were very hard working. The father did so well that they became millionaires. However, things suddenly changed when the son was still a minor, and got his girlfriend pregnant. When this dilemma occurred, the parents quickly shifted monies out of the son's name, trying to protect their assets. Then, they threatened their son and told him that if he married the girl, he would lose all of his inheritance. He had to literally deny that he had ever been involved with the girl. To make matters worse, she lived next door to them. She had to sue him and have a trial to prove that he was the father of her baby.

---

[26] 2 Peter 3:9

[27] Philippians 2:12

Their response to their situation went against many things in the Word of God. People are destroyed for lack of knowledge[28] and this is definitely what occurred here. Their response showed that money was more important than people. The Word says that you can serve God or you can serve money. [29] They put their son in parochial school but did not follow with God's principles when this situation faced them. They taught him it was acceptable to lie rather than face a situation with honesty. Lastly, it went against the principle that children are a blessing from the Lord. [30]

This son learned he had no true foundation to stand on. He turned to drugs, spent years working at low-paying jobs, while his parents again and again offered to give him financial support to help him get his Master's degree, open an expensive restaurant, whatever he wanted. He said no. He just lived life and his first marriage failed.

The curse of sin in any situation causes difficulties that don't usually affect one person, but they come down and affect others. There are blessings of up to 1,000 generations for us if we do the right things. The cursings go down as far as four generations. You can see how the curse of death operates. This Scripture is from the Old Testament but we have a greater covenant with Christ. The anointing of Jesus Christ, which is the power of God, comes in and destroys the yoke, or bondage that is on us.[31] "...And I give unto them eternal life; and they shall never perish, neither shall any man pluck them out of my hand.[32]"

Each and every choice we make in life is important. Death affects all of us. My husband and I have suffered a difficult experience with our own oldest

---

[28] Hosea 4-6

[29] Matthew 6:24

[30] Isaiah 44:3

[31] Isaiah 10:27

[32] John 10:28

daughter. We serve a God who is faithful and we stand on His Word to have good results. Please stand with us as we know all things work together for good to them that love God.[33] The great thing about Jesus is that he takes our mess and works it all out for good. We don't need to stay in death. We don't need to be strong. We are strong in our weakness.[34] We are amazing in our broken-ness. That is what our God does. We discover from our death, from our unsaved life, from our errors, our mistakes, just how much we need Jesus. All of us make mistakes. All of us fall short. As we come into a deeper and deeper relationship with Him, we realize just how much we are in need of a Savior. So, God takes the last (those of us who led very troubled lives) and makes them first.[35] He takes the ones the world casts in the ditch and puts them in his loving arms and remakes them, remolds them, and pours a mountain of love inside of them so that they can help others discover this love. He takes the ones who serve Him and follow Him and gives them more and more, greater and greater, as they walk and develop a deeper relationship with Him. To the ones who receive more of the kingdom of God, more is required of them. The Scripture says, "To whom much is given, much is required."[36]

As we are built up, we must fight the good fight of faith. We must stand up to what is dead, but stand up with the love of Jesus Christ, not the hatred and anger so prevalent in the world we live in. We all have to learn this, whether we are coming from the direction of the Church, being called to go out and help find the lost and bring them into a deep relationship with Christ, as well as those of us lost and coming into the kingdom. We need to come and leave our dead stuff behind because we are new creations in Christ, old things are passed away and all things are made new![37]

---

[33] Romans 8:28

[34] 2 Corinthians 12:9

[35] Matthew 19:30

[36] Luke 12:48

Now, we'll move into looking at how we affect what is dead in our culture and in the church. What is not God has been able to bulldoze its way into much of the Church. We have to balance the sin-covering eye with the one that will stand up to turn over the tables as Jesus did when the money changers were outside of the temple. He did this because what He saw was abhorrent to God. If we don't speak up for righteousness, then more and more ground is taken by the enemy. The enemy comes right inside the Church to divide us and keep us where we are powerless to affect our world. The dead are pushing the dead agenda – and we have to leave the dead behind.

How do we stand up to the dead? They are like the Egyptians, whose bones have been decaying our culture for centuries. They erect these big monstrosities right in our midst and call them the greatest wonders of the earth: temples dedicated to other gods; a media that worship teenagers who receive instant fame and then, crumble right before our eyes; the numbers of the killing of unborn children that are at staggering levels. The world surrounding us is as lost as ancient Egypt was. We have numerous people who truly believe if they are just good, but do not have Jesus, they will go to heaven. They are dead, but believe they get all the benefits that are contrary to the Word of God. So, how do we stand up to this?

The answer is simple.

It's so simple you might miss it.

We must get the death out of us, so we can show others how to get the death out of them. What is the death inside of us? It's separation from God.

How do we keep from being separated from God? We must learn God's truths. We must learn what our Word says and stand on it. We must get in the midst of hearing the Word of God spoken that we will grow in our faith. We must come together and build fellowship as we grow in Christ. We must step

[37] 2 Corinthians 5:17

out of our comfort zone and support what God is doing. We must encourage our children to pursue every area of life and take it for the kingdom of God. We must not turn our back on the world, but go in fully committed and be a light in the darkness. Let's be fearful of becoming lukewarm because we received our blessing and ask God to help us become on fire with Him.

Let's leave behind the dead:

• In our culture	• In our families	• In our places of work
• In our churches	• In our choices	• In our reputations
• In our popularity	• In our homes	• In our security

Let's turn the statement that Jesus gives us about that we might have life and have it more abundantly and turn it into "We MUST have life and have it more abundantly." Then, let's share our faith with others. Let's not rest in the assembly of the dead but get right in the midst of understanding.

Okay, I thought I was reading a book about TREASURE you say. And you just spent the last chapter showing me how I am treasure. So, why all of this

> A man who wanders from the way of understanding
> will rest in the assembly of the dead.
> Proverbs 21:16

death? Well, the good thing is that it's not your fault. We must remember that we came into a world that was fallen. Let's stay the course and get to where we want to get to so that God can help us to be BIGGER and BETTER TREASURE.

We need to look at what is dead. When something is dead, what do we do with it? We bury it. It begins to smell. It begins to decay. So, it must be hidden under the dirt or the dogs will dig it up. Isn't this like the things we've done in our past? Just when we think the dead things, the things that we want to leave behind in our pasts are finally out of our lives – BAM! They begin to stink. Someone says something and out BURSTS that dead thing! How did all this death come upon us? Let's go back to the beginning and see what the word says.

In the garden of Eden, God gave Adam one rule:[38]

There was death and life, right in front of Adam. God created this amazing place and breathed life into Adam. God placed part of Himself inside His creation but when Adam chose to take in death, which again is separation from

> And the Lord God commanded the man, saying, of every tree of the garden thou mayest freely eat: But of the tree of the knowledge of good and evil, thou shalt not eat of it: for in the day that thou eatest thereof thou shalt surely die.

God, he received death.

Do you remember what it felt like without God?

It was death.

Adam unwisely and unknowingly chose to follow death and so, through all generations there are those on the planet are walking around dead. I have literally seen gray shadows covering people, even children, as death covers them

[38] Geneisis 2:16-17

when they are not saved and there is some level of darkness showing up in their lives. When we choose Christ, we choose to live. We are choosing to come back under that covering, that life which never ends with God.

We must determine what is dead, what is part of that dead life and get rid of it. To do this effectively, four things need to happen. First, we receive our salvation. This is the first part of the journey. We get the water baptism, which is symbolic for the death and burial of the old man and the resurrection of the new. Second, we receive the infilling of the Holy Spirit. This is the transformation experience whereby God comes and lives inside of us, with signs and wonders following. Third, we step into our inheritance as sons and daughters of God. This step-by-step transformation God does in us. He leads us. He prompts us. He shows us as He comes to walk with us. We are now going to do this forever. It's going to go on and on and on. It is called eternity.

As a side note, God once revealed to me that heaven was like the movie 'Ground Hog's Day'. Did you ever see that? Well, in the movie, the main character has to keep repeating the same day over and over until he gets it right. At first, the character is very selfish but as he continues day after day, he changes into a much nicer person, helping others and experiencing this one day that he has to live, again and again. Our main character goes from being a jerk into becoming a guy we really, really like. He's not perfect but he comes up higher and higher each time he lives the same day.

Here on earth, we can change every day we experience with God and easily get right if we are saved. There are four simple things we need to do:

FOUR EASY STEPS TO FREEDOM

1) Sincerely say you're sorry to God for what you did.

2) Ask God to help you with this area in your life.

3) Forgive yourself and move on.

4) Fill up with the Word of God, fellowship and meditation.

Wow. That's almost too easy. Yet, that's the God we serve. He wants it to be easy for us because he wants us to live like we are in the Garden of Eden and walk with Him in the cool of the day. Remember, there is no condemnation to those of us that are in Christ Jesus.[39] We are to come to Christ as little children.[40] This is just how a little kid would do it. Also, the Holy Spirit is the one who will bring to you the part of death you are to get rid of. So, allow the Lord to show you rather than some person who sees what you need done. God is gentle and He loves us through allowing the Holy Spirit to help us get rid of what is dead.

You may still ask how do I move on? When death continues to riddle you – you must start filling up with something else. You must fill up with God. You see, it says if we are *in* Christ Jesus. How do you fill up? You need the Word. You need to fellowship with other believers. You need to meditate on God's word, which means to sit and think about what God has spoken and allow it to come into your heart.

The process leads to the fact that you empty out and He comes inside you. You must replace what is dead with what is alive. This is such an important element that Jesus told a parable about it. You see, if you try and go back to death, it comes on seven times stronger.[41] Jesus talks about a man who gets an

---

[39] Romans 8:1

[40] Mark 10:15

[41] Matthew 12:43-45

unclean spirit out of him. The man is now dry. He needs to fill up with God. He has left behind what was evil but there's nothing in there. If he continues on his way, without getting God into those places, it leaves room for "seven other spirits more wicked than himself to come and move inside of him." I believe Jesus is giving us this example to show us just how important it is for us to fill up with God inside of where it was dead.

For me, death is my past. I made lots of bad choices and decisions along the way that allowed a lot of junk to get on me. It still pops up and I have to follow those four steps. I'm sorry. I ask for help. I receive forgiveness and I fill up with the Word.

LOOK FOR PEACE

Remember, Satan promises you treasure, but it leads to despair and destruction. He promised Jesus all the kingdoms of the world but Jesus came back with the Word as life.[42] How do you know if you've left the dead behind? You will have peace. If you don't feel that presence of peace, no matter what your circumstances are, you aren't following Jesus.

I know a woman that is on a hamster wheel. Her hamster's name is Worry. When I speak with her, around and around she goes on the wheel, as fast as she can. One of my church elders has told me that worry is the interest that you pay on the problem of tomorrow. She lives chasing this future that will never take her anywhere good. Her thought life has created a lot of physical pain in her body. She would talk to me for hours about all the things she was worrying about. I tried to help but she'd made this hamster Worry, which is a close friend of Death, her best friend. I couldn't get a word in edge-wise before this friend Worry, would have to interrupt. Do not make Death and his friends, Worry, Fear and Despair, your friends. I gave this woman some Spiritual teaching tapes that I had found useful. Then, the Lord even spoke to me about what her

[42] Matthew 3:9-10

problem was so that I could pray for her. She didn't trust God. Notice how the exact opposite spirit of Worry is Trust. She needed to let go and trust God. She was spending so much time listening and speaking to her friend Worry that she had forgotten to listen to the very best friend she could ever have, Jesus Christ who tells us to cast our cares on Him, give Him our problems and He will give us rest.[43]

It's a continuous thing, spending time with God and filling up with Him. It is critical that we make sure we go through the process to get rid of death in our lives so that we can have the life that Jesus has died to give us. If we are to truly be on this treasure hunt with God, we're going to have to let go of the former things, things that are dead and follow Christ.

Let's forget what is behind and let's press into what is ahead. God is not a God of the dead, things that cause us to be separated from Him. He is a God of life![44] Once we have Christ, we can't die anymore and we are equal to the angels and are the children of God, the children of resurrection.[45] We have been literally given back our lives, the eternal ones. That is what Jesus does in us. However, since God gives us free will, Jesus will only take what we give to Him.

[43] Matthew 11:28

[44] Luke 20:38

[45] Luke 20:36

TREASURE

CHAPTER THREE

PRECIOUS METALS

God gave them gold –

but man without God began worshipping the gold

rather than the God who gave it to them.

How we are like gold, as we are purified to become like God.

WE MUST BE PUT IN THE FIRE

Do you like stuff? Do you like flashy, shiny objects that glisten and twinkle? I'm not one for jewelry, but at one point I had a beautiful ring with numerous diamonds. I wore it with a black watch and several shiny silver bracelets. One of the production assistants I worked with began calling me 'magpie' because my hand attracted attention. It was shining. We shouldn't feel bad about liking jewelry and shiny objects. Remember, God made them and the streets of heaven are paved with gold. However, we must not be like the magpie. A magpie is attracted to anything that is shiny, whether it is of any true value or not. As believers in Christ, we must develop our levels of discernment to be able to distinguish between what is of real value and what looks shiny but is of no value. This is the difference between what God shows us that has lasting value and what the world promises us is valuable. We can't chase the flashing, fleeting, momentary thing. What's the difference you ask? The world's offers don't last. They shine. Yet, with the world's things, their moments of pleasure are quickly over and we are still left with the desire unfulfilled. This is because

God built us to hold much more than the possessions of the world. We are built to hold Him.

Let's remember to get things in perspective. God put the gold in heaven under our feet. We are to be above it, not to worship it. Building our foundations on what is GOLD (i.e. of true value) we must be put this under us to walk on, stand on and move in. We cannot take it up and begin worshipping it. That's what so irritated God. Why are you worshipping what I have given you – and why do you think you should pray to it? [46] They could value the gold in their hands – but when it became the center of what they wanted, and they discerned that a piece of metal was what was of true value, God became angry because they lost sight of what was of real value: a relationship with Him.

God is beyond being made in *our* image. He is beyond what we can control. He is bigger than anything that we are. When Moses had been gone too long in the wilderness, up on the mountain with God, people quickly forgot and created something they thought was worthy to worship. We cannot make Him an object we can control. God takes us and forms us, and puts us into the heat, like gold to see what we are made of. We can't do the same to Him.

As we become the treasure of God, we will be put through our own set of journeys. How do we know what will happen to us? In our map, the Holy Bible, God lays out several things or processes that we will go through as we go with Him. First, we encounter the love affair. This is the point when we have had that God encounter like Jacob had. We must have this in order to be truly saved in Christ. There will be a transformation in us, an infilling of God's Spirit into us and we will know we are saved.

Next, we will begin our journey. How long this part takes is up to God's plan for our lives, and how we react to the tests that are placed before us. It's a combination of our lives, and it's all Scriptural. Generational curses and

---

[46] Read Exodus 32

blessings are involved. What do we need to have taken out of us before God can begin really filling things in? This could be described as our wilderness experience. It's the journey that officially was to take 11 days but took 40 years. I have met Christians who have been in that place for 20 years. I have met some that have never allowed God that much access to their lives, and so they seem blessed in their outer lives but their inner lives have not gotten very far in the process. They are always trying to fill up on the outside because the inside is so empty.

Once God truly becomes the center and core of your life, when you are completely His, and you have turned back no more, He begins the journey up the mountain. This is the walk like Moses took. You enter places with God and heights that you never knew existed, as He unfolds the mysteries that belong to Him alone that He wants to share with you.

The Lord has levels to each mountain. The first one He led me up had seven levels. After that, He told me I was stepping into ministry and I began immediately to be on prophetic teams prophesying to groups of people. The Spirit would drop on me at times and the Lord would direct who I spoke to and would flow out with words of edification, exhortation, comfort and direction. If you don't feel anywhere near this, remember, God is no respecter of persons[47] and He uses the foolish to confound the wise and the weak to confound the mighty.[48] God loves to make the underdog the hero. He loves to take the absolutely last person you'd ever think would be who God would pick and use them. So, do not by any means count yourself out!

God showed me that there are other mountains ahead of that mountain, for it is ceaseless where God will take you as you walk into deeper places with Him.

---

[47] Acts 10:34

[48] 1 Corinthians 1:27

I saw where others who had been walking with the Lord were up on higher mountains, overcoming greater tests than mine.

On this journey, you will need to take some things with you. You continue to surrender all of you to Him so that He can fill you with what He is. This is why we are referred as being put into the fire so that we will come out as gold. Just as God stopped living in temples that were made by human hands and came inside of us, the gold that God wants to create here on earth is us. We are what is most valuable to Him. God brings the fire into our lives to burn out what is not gold in us. When God brings in the fire, He does not mess around. He brings fire and it can devastate us but if we turn toward God in the midst of the fire, we can come out gold.

Let's look at Peter in the third chapter in the Book of Acts. Let's see how God intervenes in a man's fire. In this passage of Scripture, there is a man who has no use of his legs and is begging at the Gate Beautiful. The word Beautiful here[49] means belonging to the right hour or season, something that is timely. This man has been put in the fire. It does not say how this man came to having lost the use of his legs, and having lost any way to make a living. He may have been born that way. He may have not followed the path of righteousness and through a series of mistakes came to the end of himself. The Bible doesn't tell us how the man got there but there he was. He was crippled and begging.

However, he was crying out at the right time because Peter was walking by. He was in the right location, at the Gate Beautiful. The time was in the 9th hour. This was the time to birth something. The man asked for the wrong thing. He asked from the place of his need rather than the place of what he had the right to access. He was begging rather than receiving. He did what he could to just get by.

---

[49] Strong's Concordance Greek 5611, root 5610

How many of us just get by with what we think God has given us? How many of us just accept the little we have rather than press into what is not working in our lives, and get down to our situations so we can have access to more of what God has, and wants to give us? How many of us are afraid of the fire we might have to journey through to come out as gold? There is a price for more, but oh, is it well worth it!

Our crippled beggar asked for money.

Oh, if we can get this Scripture, we can move into some great places as God's Treasure. You see, God's Word tells us that he will give us the power to get wealth.[50] We still have to do the work to get this power. Power in the Hebrew of my Strong's Concordance means to be firm, have vigor, force, capacity, means, produce, also ability, might, power, strength, substance and wealth. Amazingly, wealth in the Hebrew means force, an army, wealth, virtue, valor, strength, activity, forces, goods, host, might, power, riches, substance and virtue. God gives us the ability, strength and substance to get an army, wealth, and riches. You cannot reap a harvest without first planting the field. If you do your part, God will do His part. The key in this is to seek the kingdom first, and His righteousness, and all these things will be added unto you.[51]

We need to seek the kingdom first, seek righteousness, peace and joy in the Holy Ghost first, and to be right with God (which we learn from His Word), and God will add everything to us. He'll add the abilities, the substance, the strength, the power, the wealth, the riches, the virtue, the forces and armies, the activity…all of it. God will add it.

When we are in the fire, we need to take God's solutions. We need to learn of God's ways. Peter was sent to this man to start him on the journey as he was in the fire of testing.

---

[50] Deuteronomy 8:18

[51] Matthew 6:33

Then, Peter said, "...silver and gold have I none; but such as I have give I thee: in the name of Jesus Christ of Nazareth rise up and walk."[52] Peter didn't have cold, hard cash on hand, he had something even greater. Peter had power. He went right to the source of the problem and fixed it. This is what God is about when He gets into our lives. He is willing to take us on journeys through the wilderness, through our valleys, and as we grow in Him, up mountains, in order to solve our problems rather than just temporarily solving our symptoms by a quick fix. We must mature in seeking the kingdom in order to receive all.

If we receive the stuff, the blessings without the ability to handle it, we are doomed. We will enter the trials and tests and we can get burned. How much better it is to ask God to give us what we can handle, and to prepare us for more so that we can receive it.

I was a model, presentation person when I was young. I received a lot of attention, and I was not prepared in the slightest for it in the areas of inner strength. The entire experience blew me up. After a horrific journey getting back to a right balance, I prayed a prayer, not really knowing God was listening. I said out loud, "God don't ever give me something I cannot handle." God listened. The only times I have been blown up since that time was when I disregarded the Holy Spirit in me, checking me, to let me know it wasn't the best He had for me. I would rather wait a life time, asking to be prepared, than to step into the fiery furnace and get burned. The fires get very hot in life. The fires can destroy us. Let's ask to go in and come out without an ounce of smoke, with the Son of Man at our side.

We must gain in our understanding of what it means to be inside the Word of God and get our faith built up strong. Then, we really begin to be treasure to God. Without faith it is impossible to please God.[53] Maybe you don't feel like

---

[52] Acts 3:6

[53] Hebrews 11:6

you have faith. I know that at times, when God's Spirit is flowing inside of me, I feel so full of faith that I could speak to the earth and feel it move. Yet, there are other times when I feel so low that I couldn't muster up a word of faith at all. That's what this process is about. God takes us in and out of the fire, refining us, burning out what is not Him, bringing up what we need to work on and build in our lives, so that He can fill us with more and more of Him.

How do we go through these tests?

I am finding that there are some things that really help. Get around believers. I don't mean the kind which are more concerned with their parties than their prayer life.[54] I mean the kind of believers who you can trust, who have walked through trials, who won't judge you, who you can count on, and who you see fruit in their deep walk with God. Find those believers and ask God to show you who they are, and then, ask them for prayer. The prayers of a righteous man avail much. [55] You want someone who is knocking on heaven's door and can actually get in!

Then, remember that Jesus is the author and finisher of our faith! [56] He is the one who went to the cross for our sin. He is the one who can help us as we run this race of faith in order to be pleasing to God.

Listen to the instruction:

> My son, do not despise the chastening of the Lord;
>
> Neither be weary of His correction;
>
> For whom the Lord loves He corrects...
>
> Proverbs 3: 11-12

If we weren't of value to God, we wouldn't be put into

---

[54] This is a reference back to Exodus 32

[55] James 5:16

[56] Hebrews12:1-2

these tests. The two things we receive from this are becoming a person who receives holiness, and a person who receives righteousness.[57] We begin to enter inside the gates of the kingdom and into the reality of the kingdom as we become holy. We develop in our love walk with our Creator and He develops us, teaching us how to be close to Him.

Listen to the promise in Hebrews 12:5-6 that was made about what God was going to do when He sent His Son Jesus to be our Savior. Jesus changes us and transforms us, and molds us and makes us into the image that God had planned for our lives. He just needs our willingness, our openness to receive Him into our lives.

I remember the first year we moved across the country when we were filled with the Spirit of the Lord. My heart cried out so many times to go home. California was not an Egypt to me. God had blessed me mightily there. Yet, over a period of years, I learned that Satan would use this to get me off course. God used it to test me. As I stayed where the Lord had me, I went through many years of isolation. We went through many years where the Lord would not release me to get a regular job and John was doing all sorts of odd jobs in between his music playing dates. We had times where we had two days worth of food in the pantry and we didn't know what was going to happen next. In my dreams, the rural townspeople in our small southern town appeared as Vietnamese to me. They were that foreign to me. Yet, with time, the place of my captivation became the place of God's release over my life. As I was isolated, the hunger for more of God through his Word, through Christian TV, and spending time with Him became my fortress. He answered my prayers and poured out many secret things to me because I was available and there weren't the normal distractions. I was literally a captive audience. Soon, I know the place he had me was set up so that He and I would come together. As I poured

---

[57] Hebrews 12:10 - 11

out, He poured in. The Words of His Revelation poured into me. I had moments of spiritual ecstasy with heaven coming in so powerfully to my house, completely filled with His Presence.

Now, I still yearn for my homeland of California but I yearn to be in God's will more. I yearn to be used by Him, be in His Presence, and help others. He now hands back my homeland, where I will be able to reside several months a year but I only want to go if He is going before me. Moses felt this way when he told God, if God's Presence wasn't going, Moses didn't want to go.[58] The fire was to stay where God had placed me, through storms and isolation, financial tests and difficulties, and learn to press inside of the Lord at levels I may have never reached had I not walked this way.

In life's meltdowns, we are supposed to be learning how to engage with Him. We learn how to 'rise above it' and soon, the tests we encounter don't seem as difficult. We melt down and harden again. Each time we are a little stronger, a little more qualified, because the thing we must remember is that we are being prepared to fight the good fight of faith[59] here so we can redeem rewards in heaven.

Moses had learned the important ingredient. Why would we want to be anywhere the Lord isn't in our lives? He sifts us, purifies us, remolds us, and then, as something much greater and more valuable we re-emerge and we are useful. This change in us, where we would prefer to be in bondage but with God, allows God to melt us into truly being His treasure. What happens is that His treasures, His secret mysteries, are revealed to us and He sends the kingdom, those amazing streets of gold, down and we walk on them with Him. We are priceless, precious, valuable treasure to God. The Lord shows us more

---

[58] Exodus 33:15

[59] I Timothy 6:12

and more of Him because we have proven ourselves worthy with what He has given us.

God knows just the temperature we can take and the desires, the real desires of our hearts. He knows just how to get us there. The Word says He'll bring us through the fire and refine us like silver and try us like gold and we will call on Him and He will hear us and He'll say we're His people and we'll say the Lord is our God.[60]

How do we do this? We must recognize the parts of us that need God and repent so that we can have what God promises us.[61] We must trust Him in the process, and surrender to His will along the way. If we can't trust Him, we haven't spent enough time with Him to know who He is. We learn in the fiery trials who He is. We learn how Jesus will never leave us nor forsake us.[62] Never. He was right there in the fiery furnace and they weren't burnt because of the trust they developed in Him.[63]

Working hard to learn what God has to teach us in these trials is worth it – and we come out as gold. We put all of our possessions – the things we value – on the altar. God then takes what we have and gives us back so much more!

Join with me in this prayer out loud.

God, search my heart.

If there is anything I need to put on the altar,

Please show me!

---

[60] Zecheriah 13:9

[61] Revelations 3:18

[62] Hebrews 13:5

[63] Daniel 3

TREASURE

CHAPTER FOUR

TEMPLES and THEIR CONSTRUCTION

We are to be the Temples of God.

God likes places He can occupy.

Look at how much fighting there is

over the Temple Mount in Jerusalem.

Think of how much more warfare

is happening over you.

IT'S IMPORTANT THAT WE HOLD GOD IN US

A while back, I visited a large Methodist church and I stood over the rotunda. A little boy was on the lower floor, wild and fidgeting as his mother corrected him and told him, "Behave. This is God's house." The little boy answered matter-of-factly, "No, it's not. It's the Church." His little mind had not given God a residence and he was actually right.

When Jesus came, the veil was torn in the temple and God's presence left. Then, at Pentecost, the Spirit returned and came inside of us. We are the temples of God. That little boy was shaking his temple, and his temple hit his mother's building. We could say a little earthquake was happening.

In Greece, a few years back, the Associated Press reported that the police seized thousands of artifacts and treasures and arrested a man. They called what he had in his possession "an ancient treasure trove." The man, a 40-year-old hairdresser, was arrested because you must carry a special permit to own, buy, sell or excavate antiquities.[64] He didn't have a permit.

God is like this, too. If you are going to carry His special treasure, you must carry a special permit, salvation. It's your admission into the kingdom. It is Christ within you. You must have repented, taken Jesus Christ as your Savior and become born of water and of the Spirit.[65] This is what occurs for you to become the temple of God. You are literally a regenerated being and this occurrence gives you the permission to belong to God as His treasure. You have received the most important relationship there ever was.

Now, let's imagine something. Picture a building in your mind. It is red brick and is fresh, new and is seven stories tall. It has many entrances and exits. It has hundreds of windows where the sun shines in. Laughter fills the hallways, and much work is completed within its walls. All sorts of life, ideas, work, relationships, knowledge, activity, and friendships are formed and carried out here. It is thriving.

However, over a period of years the owner doesn't take care of the building. A window gets broken and it's not repaired. The grass in the front yard stops being mowed. No one plants any flowers one year, and then stops planting flowers at all. Cracks form in the foundation and are never repaired. The windows stop being cleaned. The whole neighborhood becomes run down and the trash piles up on the sidewalks, and the city forgets to come and pick it up.

This is like us.

We can start out as beautiful buildings, beautiful children created by God but if we aren't taken care of, if we aren't taught how to take care of ourselves, we can go astray and we do go astray.

Soon, like those buildings, we can forget that we have been made to stand seven stories tall, where our upper floors stand with the heavens and amidst the

---

[64] http://cpprot.te.verweg.com/2005-February/000730.html

[65] John 3:3-7

clouds. We were created to stand strong and powerful and to fill up with all God's treasures inside of us.

Others may see wrecked out buildings, with our windows broken and rodents scurrying behind the discarded interiors, but our God always remembers what He created. He remembers what He made, and continues to see us as beautiful in spite of how we may look to the world. You see, God has this amazing plan. He has this design for our function and its use and it's bigger and better than all we could imagine, think or ask.[66]

God is a creator. He created all that is in this world, in this universe that continues to get larger and expand, as well as life so small we can't see it but can only guess how it is formed.

This God who has made everything sees us as a beautiful building no matter what we look like. He sees us as a place He'd like to move into. God wants to take our broken down buildings, empty them out and fill them up with Him. He wants to wash our windows so we see clearly. He wants to plant beautiful things right at our feet. He wants us to look out from places high, high in the sky and see what it looks like from heaven's point of view.

Look at this next Scripture and see what God does with us when we accept Him and accept His offer to allow Him to change us:

---

[66] Ephesians 3:20

Does this not describe a building in disrepair, long over-looked and forgotten? Yet, Jesus regenerates us. This word regenerate means: we are spiritually changed in our character and habits, or that we are revived and given a new life.[67]

> We were also once foolish, disobedient, deceived, serving various lusts and pleasures, living in malice and envy, hateful and hating one another. But when the kindness and the love of God our Savior toward man appeared, not by the works of righteousness which we have done, but according to His mercy He saved us, thoroughly washing of regeneration and renewing of the Holy Spirit, whom He poured out on us abundantly through Jesus Christ our Savior.
>
> Titus 3:3-6 NKJV

The Maker of heaven and earth knows He doesn't make junk. If you feel like this, ask Him to clean you out, ask Him to take what has been able to move into your building and get it out. Ask Him to empty you out and show you how He sees you – as beautiful treasure, as a temple on a hill, seven stories high, reflecting the light that has been put inside of you, ready to receive and hold the treasure He wants you and only you to carry.

This is what it means to become the temple of God. We are changed from a building that holds our 'stuff' into temples that hold treasure as God takes His

---

[67] Webster's Dictionary

Word, gives it life and puts heaven inside of us. We receive the special permit to carry treasure and receive the kingdom. Since the kingdom is righteousness, peace and joy in the Holy Spirit,[68] these outward signs and inward rewards come into us and we can do what God says and be like Him, full of love, mercy and kindness, slow to anger,[69] not demanding our own way, because love cannot fail.[70]

Let's remember, we are the temples of God. Know ye not that ye are the temple of God, that the Spirit of God dwelleth in you? [71] Now that we've established that you are the temple, let's move into what God does with temples.

God loves temples. He loves churches and places that are dedicated to Him. If you look at the amount of time He put into building a temple He could reside inside of that Solomon built,[72] it's amazing. Yet God left the building because He had created a way He could reside inside of us. Men in Israel are fighting over this place, this location where God's Presence once was in residence. Yet, God left the building.

We shouldn't be as concerned about where God was. We should be concerne
d   with
where
God   is
and
where He
is going!

---

[68] Romans 14:17

[69] Nehemiah 9:17

[70] 1 Corinthians 13:8

[71] I Corinthians 3:16

[72] 1 Kings 6

God told his people. The messenger here is referring to John the Baptist and the Lord's temple that we come to is Jesus Christ.[73] Jesus inside of us makes us the temple.

God warned Israel and said, "…Return to me and I will return unto you…"

TAKE CARE OF THE TEMPLE THAT WE ARE

As the temples of God, now that we have our permit in proper order, we can take care of our temple in three ways.

1) Take care of our own bodies. We must be responsible for how we are taking care of our bodies. Our diet. Our choices. Our purity.

2) Take care of our immediate families, friends, neighbors, those close to us that God has put into our lives.

3) Take care of our relationships within the body of Christ – are we

> Behold, I will send my messenger,
> and he shall prepare the way before me:
> And the Lord, whom you seek,
> shall suddenly come to His temple…
> Malachi 3:1

ready at anytime for God to return? Are we in our assignment, in our temple, ready for God to use us? Are we placed where God

---

[73] John 2:19-2:21

wants us or are we fighting the direction He is trying to take us? Have we made sure we are not offended?[74]

If we can say yes to these three things, or that we are moving in this direction, let's move on and assess where we are in our becoming treasure. You have gotten rid of what is dead and allowed yourself to endure tests. What is next in our journey of treasure hunting? Remember the five things we would encounter: : 1) the risk of death; 2) leaving behind comfort of what was normal and safe; 3) not doing things by a religious 'legalistic' rule system; 4) the promise of adventure; 5) the promise of amazing riches.

How can we accomplish the task of treasure hunting if we haven't begun to build something the treasure would go in? God wants us to be responsible about our temple – the body that He comes inside of. Remember, it's Jesus who changes our vile body into being glorious.[75]

How?

Little by little. Yet, there are ways to accelerate this process. First, we're told to love the Lord with all our heart, soul and mind.[76] God doesn't want a little of us, although He will accept that for a time. He wants all of us. We are all the body of Christ.[77]

We have to get control over how we are speaking and our thought life as the temples of God. Death and life are in the power of the tongue.[78] If we can get our mouths working right, then God can get into our situation. We've got to chase down our tongues and get them under control so God can begin pouring

---

[74] Luke 7:23

[75] Philippians 3:21

[76] Matthew 22:37

[77] 1 Corinthians 2:27

[78] Proverbs 18:21

in Christ – where God is. We have to find a way to where God is. We have to get rid of what isn't God because no flesh will glory in His presence.[79] If we want more of God, we have to give up our habits and ways, and replace them with His ways. Remember, we all fall short. If you want His ways and you've been missing it, then just tell Him you're sorry and remember there's joy in the presence of the angels for what you are doing![80]

Now, let's look at a thing most of us heard as children:

Sticks and stones will break your bones

but words will never hurt you.

This is a basic lie.

I remember before my son, Dakota's eyes were healed by the Lord, he was a little second grader with some pretty thick glasses. A group of 4 or 5 younger boys taunted Dakota and he retaliated. My little second grader punched a few of these first graders back and they ran away.

The words that these children said caused an attack because my son did not believe what they were saying. It angered him. It came completely against what he was being taught to believe. As a child, like we are all supposed to be in God, Dakota believed God's Word completely. Every night my husband John would pray with Dakota to receive that healing in his eyes. What if Dakota had stopped believing that God was going to do what His Word said? He would still be in thick glasses, where his eyes would never be completely healed rather than walking freely without them.

Now, I am not encouraging you to take matters into your own hands in the physical retaliation like Dakota did with these boys. We learn how to fight off the bullies in the Spirit. Yet, we must stand up to what is wrong, and learn how

[79] 1 Corinthians 1:29

[80] Luke 15:10

to do it in Christ. As believers, we must become gold in how we operate using those fruits of the Spirit. My son was a little guy and didn't know how to take down principalities in the Spirit but he did know how to defend himself from attack. He was in a public school, a place with no covering since prayer was removed from the schools. He was on the front lines and did what he thought was best at the time. I stood at his back, like God would stand at my back, as he stood up to the enemy of words that assaulted him. The boys at school didn't make fun of him after that. He had stood up to them and held his ground. He didn't get into any other fights. Then, God healed Dakota's eyes and he won over the enemy!

What tests do you face? What bullies do you encounter? What miracles of God are you waiting for? What promises are you standing on? What kinds of assaults are trying to destroy your temple?

We must, as mature believers recognize that Christ is the cornerstone to what we are built on. If we want power we have to learn God's ways to operate. So, first we have to get our legs to stand where Christ is. We have to build our foundation on Him. How do we do this? We get into His Word. We learn how to operate in heavenly principles rather than earthly ones. We learn in this world to hear no evil. We learn how in this world to see no evil. We learn how in this world to speak no evil. By managing our senses, and more importantly, how we respond to what we are seeing in the natural and learn to respond the way heaven wants us to respond, we can keep ourselves from enemy attack and then, we can begin to embrace the power that is Christ in us.

Here are some elements of temples. Temples need inner courts. You must establish a secret place for you to be alone with God. You must create time to spend with Him. You must grow in the places you spend with Him and He will plant things, like a garden inside of your heart that He comes and waters. He will put in roses and palm trees and will dance with you in these private places.

If you don't do what's necessary to have a great temple, you will have a cold temple, or one that needs to have the weeds that have grown up taken down.

Why do you need a temple?

As treasure you need something to put treasure inside of.

Enemies try and steal treasure. The enemy we face is subtle.[81] We must create a strong house to put our faith inside of so that when that enemy tries to come, we have built such a strong place for what we know, believe and hold, that he can't get in. As we walk with the Lord, we learn to close every door, every window, and every crack to the enemy. We do this by putting our eyes directly on Jesus and not letting go. If your eyes are focused on what is happening in heavenly places, then the things of this world take on their proper perspective. You can stand as a temple no matter what hits you.

Temples are made of strong stuff. Their foundations are solid. They withstand attack, change and storms. They withstand attack from enemies as well as friends. This means that the circumstances in our lives might change: our finances, our governments, our lives- but our God, He does not change. He's the same today, yesterday and forever.[82] The storms we encounter, the things we don't expect in life will come. Yet Jesus was in the boat sleeping when the storm hit. All who were with Him thought they were going to die and it seemed like Jesus was there asleep. Yet, when Jesus awoke, it just took one word from God's mouth and all was solved.[83] Jesus expects us to go through attack, change and storms, but as we become the temple that God comes inside of and dwells, we learn how to be filled with God, and therefore, the things that are not of God cannot rest there.

---

[81] 2 Corinthians 11:3

[82] Hebrews 13:8

[83] Mark 4

So, how do we separate ourselves from the things swirling around us and press into being with God? If you say the tests are too hard, then, listen to what a woman can truly go through if she wants to get alone with God. There are stories about John Wesley's mother Susanna who had 19 children and would take her apron over her head in order to obtain prayer time.[84] She had to push everything away and be inside of the strong temple that she had built. Is your situation greater than raising up 19 children? Somehow under the sanctuary of her apron, Susanna made a way to go into the temple so she could do what she needed to do. Her son, John, was the founder of numerous denominations. So, out of her belly flowed the river of living water[85] and what Jesus gave her poured out onto her son. She was quite a temple this mother of 19 kids! Susanna Wesley was a determined woman to go after God this way. Our persistence to go after God and what builds us is central to having a strong temple.

Let's rejoice as we remember, we are the TEMPLES OF GOD!

We have the permit to gain access to everything heaven has.

We are righteous and holy.

We walk with the King and stand in the courts of the Most High.

Let's remember, our temple is a place God created for us to rest in power. We lay down our power, or what we think is power and God pours in His power. His power is in the Spirit and it over-rides the earth's power. It supersedes it. Not by might, nor by power but by My Spirit says the Lord of Hosts.[86] On the day when Jesus died for our sin, God ripped away the veil – and He did this because He no longer lived in temples made by the hands of

---

[84] http://www.anchorlife.org/html/plact.htm also in
http://chrysaliscom.blogspot.com/2007/02/spotlight-on-mom-susannah-wesley.html

[85] John 7:38

[86] Zechariah 4:6

men, as He did in the Old Testament. He now moved His residence into the places of men. He can live in us and we truly are God's temple.[87]

As God's temple we get to go to receive heaven inside of ourselves.

Jesus goes into heaven for us so we can come out of dead works – and reside as temples carrying God inside of us! This is amazing to me. Amazing and wonderful that God calls us His treasure and then, puts heaven inside of us through Christ.

For Christ is not entered into the holy places made with hands, which are the figures of the true, but of heaven itself, now to appear in the presence of God for us.

Hebrews 9:24

[87] Luke 23:45

TREASURE

CHAPTER FIVE

JEWELRY and ALL A GIRL COULD ASK FOR

Adorning ourselves with what is of true beauty,

our beauty must come from heavenly places

and from a Father who loves us.

He is a Father to the fatherless.

WE MUST BE BEAUTIFUL

There is a difference between a Father and a Daddy. A Father disciplines. A Daddy loves. If one is not accustomed to the love of a Daddy, the discipline of a Father feels like abuse. God showed me how safe He was, how gentle and patient. From that place of discovering God's love for me, we began to develop a level of intimacy where I could go to Him with anything. He knew me inside and out. It was safe and I could run to Him with every situation I faced.

Over a period of years, the Lord began to show me who I was, who He saw me as. This journey was blissful and I suggest to every single believer to take all of your heart to God – the parts you are afraid He might see. The amazing part about Jesus is that He doesn't judge us. Jesus saves us. It's His love that draws us into His arms, and up into His lap to receive His embrace. Jesus tells us to come to Him as a little child.[88] He takes the child in us that might be broken or hurt and heals us. He builds us up until we are so full of Him that we can be whole. He creates a love affair and it's never ending. He takes us into a shelter with Him, a safe place and begins to reveal who He truly is to us.

---

[88] Mark 10:15

As His treasure, we discover that we are treasure to Him, we are important to God. We are worth something to Him. The more we know Him and spend time with Him, the more He reveals Himself in us – and when we see the reflection of Him in us, we see how good we are. He takes off layer after layer of what we used to adorn ourselves with: pride, hurt, loneliness, pain, power, fear, abandonment, drugs…and He puts Himself, His love inside of us.

Please take each one of these words into your spirit and search around to see if you have been wearing any of them. Do you get short tempered sometimes when you are around those who aren't up to par? Do you have feelings of hurt against anyone? Do you ache for good friends? Has anyone hurt you from your past, or even now in your present? Do you need or want to be in charge? Are you ever afraid? Do you feel like you'll be left for someone or something else? Have you had so much pain, you are turning to things to turn off that pain? You see, these kinds of things we carry in life can cause us to be weighed down by what they do to us. They become our jewels, our adornments, the things we display even if we never speak about them. As a man thinketh in his heart, so is he.[89] These are our jewels rather than God's jewels for us and we need to get rid of them.

Here is an example of what we might have to turn in as the world's jewels we are carrying and replace them with the jewels of heaven. When I briefly became homeless at 24, God provided a beautiful house for me to stay in. However, my own orphan spirit kept me on the floor rather than receiving the good thing God was giving me. I had to receive help and should have accepted the bed I was given. However, I held onto my shame rather than receive the gift of provision God was giving me. Another example of my old jewels and when I did accept a gift from God was when John and I were first walking in the grace of being Spirit-filled and the Lord had a minister and his wife give us one

---

[89] Proverbs 23:7

hundred dollars. I had to receive the money because I was hearing how God provided in ways that we might not understand, so I had to take my humiliation and place it on the altar and receive the gift of humility and provision that God was giving to me. God's value system doesn't operate the way we want it to. We have to learn to receive and accept what God wants to give us, even when it hurts our pride and brings us levels of humility we might not otherwise be able to experience.

Today I had to repent of driving a far distance to go to a nicer store rather than going to the same store that is much closer to me, where there are many broken and lost souls. I wanted the easier way, where others that were much more like me shopped and I could enjoy it. However, through another person's testimony I was convicted of my sin and will make a better effort to reach the lost for Jesus. The Lord revealed to me, when we were trying to move over to

that area, that He had placed me here. So, I will make a better effort to be where God has planted me and to reach out when He uses me. I lay down selfishness and take up selflessness.

I remember my own mother telling me a story from her childhood, where during the depression her wonderful step-father would not accept shoes for his children, even though they had none. His pride kept him from receiving what God wanted to get into his hands, or literally onto his children's feet. He was a very, very good man who came in and saved my grandmother and her three children, yet he made this error that burned into a young child's memory. My mother would not take help when it came and a pride developed in her which made it hard, almost impossible to accept help. We must humble ourselves and receive what God wants to give to us. Everything is a test. Everything here on earth is going to mean something for us when we get to heaven. We must learn God's Word so we know God's ways and can lay down our old jewels and receive the ones heaven wants to give us.

So, right now, let's allow ourselves to lay down what <u>used to be</u> our jewels and place them at Jesus' feet. Will you do this? Ask the Lord to show you something that is the old way of thinking and let Him replace it. You didn't know it was jewelry, this stuff you have been carrying around, but you may have been wearing it a long time and God wants you to take it off. Close your eyes and picture yourself laying down any feelings that you know aren't God's best for you at His feet. Picture the feet of Jesus on top of that thing, and then, crumbling underneath into dust. Now, let it be whisked away into nothingness. The ugly, harmful jewel is gone. Take a few moments to let it go. See it going away. See it being sent into a fire by Jesus where it is burnt and being completely destroyed. Then, repeat this process for any further hurts, fear, or pain that you feel because God wants to take your pain and turn it into something very precious.

This is the fire of God's love for you. God is an all-consuming fire. He is burning up what you just gave to Him and He will replace it with precious jewels. This is what the Lord wants for us. He wants us to be free. He wants us to reside in joy, in complete freedom. When God says, "For I consider that the sufferings of this present time are not worthy to be compared with the glory which shall be revealed in us."[90] He means it. The suffering we have can't compare to what God can put inside of us. We are delivered from the bondage of corruption into the glorious liberty.[91] The great news is that the Spirit helps us in all of our weaknesses.[92] God used fire by night to lead His people – because when we are in darkness, when we have made bad choices that lead us to dark places, God brings what will burn up this darkness and lead us out. His light leads us.

---

[90] Romans 8:18

[91] Romans 8:21

[92] Romans 8:26

As I wrote this, the Lord showed me an area of pride I had about being from California. When I was young, I took great pride in my looks because I hadn't been completed by my earthly father to feel valuable, I used the attention I received to gain my worth. This worth was connected to the pride I felt about being a Californian. I had to lay this at His feet and he took it and burned up a bathing suit I had bought. I even felt a check in my spirit when I purchased it – but I pressed on because I really, really wanted it and it was on sale. I absolutely love getting things on sale. The bathing suit and how it made me feel represented a piece of that old jewelry.

Remember to listen to the checks the Holy Spirit will give you. It is that little tug you feel from God. If you don't feel tugs like this, ask the Lord to reveal more of Himself to you. Those who seek the Lord with all their hearts will find Him. Jesus tells us that anyone who asks, receives and he that seeks, finds and to him that knocks, it is opened.[93] You can have a close walk with God. It is entirely up to you and how much of God you want. Then, when you get those checks to guide you, do as you do with all sin: repent, and do as the Lord leads. Remember, you can trust what God tells you to do because it will line up in the Word of God. As for me, my bathing suit went right into the trash.

Ouch. However, the Lord let me get another one later.

---

[93] Matthew 7:7-8

Let's look at how Jesus tells us about this process in His Word:

The Son of man shall send forth His angels, and they shall gather out of His kingdom all things that offend, and them which do iniquity...[94] This means that God has all sorts of ways to get you to give over what you treasure, what things have been what you've put on that are offensive to Him, or cause you to do wrong.

Then, he puts them in the refining fire.[95] And you may shed some tears (as I did) and have remorse about what you gave up. You might literally feel the pulling off of what was on you. It doesn't usually want to come off. It's like saying goodbye to a friend who you know isn't good for you, but you've formed a bond with. You do what God asks. However, your heart yearns for what was

---

Webster's Dictionary Definition

jewelry:

objects of precious metal set with gems and worn for personal adornment.

---

[94] Matthew 13:41

[95] Matthew 13:42

because somehow it fed something missing inside of you. That emptiness you are feeling from what has been taken away, or what you had to give up in order that you follow Him might feel like an empty cavern, a hole inside of you. However, God wants to fill that place with His Treasures, His goodness, His wholeness. First, you have to go through the emptying out of what wasn't God in your life. This is the refining fire. Then, listen to what Jesus says:

The righteous shine forth as the sun in the kingdom of their Father.[96]

We shine as we become right with God. We learn what is right with God, and forgive ourselves along the way for the error we made.

Something new happens. There is a special jewel that Jesus pours in. We begin to open ourselves up to what Jesus pours in: the priceless pearl. This is where we are willing to sell all we have to purchase.[97] Jesus is that pearl. He takes out the bad and pours in the good. What Jesus does is He covers our sin with His goodness. It pours on like liquid, and as more and more pours on we are drenched and covered with something good.

Let's investigate how a pearl is formed. A pearl is created by a tiny bit of sand getting inside of an oyster shell. When this piece of sand gets in, something that shouldn't be there, the oyster begins to cover it with a tear of liquid. This tear of liquid, is like the love of God over our sin. As we learned previously, the anointing of God destroys the yoke of bondage in our lives. Jesus destroys the sin. We have the memory of what occurred and can use it to help others in their sin. With the development process, the oyster continues to cover the sand with the tears until it forms a beautiful pearl. Then, as it hardens, it is a treasure.

Isn't this like us and our sin? If we allow Jesus into our situations, He will pour His love onto our sin, and we will develop into beautiful treasure. The

---

[96] Matthew 13:43

[97] Matthew 13:45-46

Bible says the gates of heaven are made of pearl.[98] So, God takes our sin, covers it and we can now enter heaven - and the heavenly places God has for us. This is the transformation we go through as we become the bride of Christ.

The Lord wants for us to become beautiful. The word beautiful means in Hebrew to be bright.[99] God wants us to be beautiful, to be bright and illuminate our beauty to others. We are to be treasure and become treasure and it takes time to develop something beautiful. So, allow God the time to develop your beauty. As this beauty develops, we are the light of the world. We are a city that is set upon a hill that cannot be hid.[100] You see, God makes us His jewels.[101] As we pour out more and more of our sin, God pours more and more of His beauty, His light, His love into us.

Remember, the first thing God made was light.[102] God says to us, "Let your light shine before men." This light is you and the jewels are the bright and shining parts of you that have allowed God to sweep into your hard places, your pain places, your hurts and empty areas, and fill them up with His qualities, love and joy and righteousness, limitless good qualities that He wants to pour inside of you. He takes you and makes you His jewels and then, He likes to show you off. God wants to show off what He is doing inside of you and you can rejoice because it's His light shining from within. He is what is being shown off, but as He does this in you, you are this jewel in His kingdom. The kingdom is righteousness, peace and joy in the Holy Ghost.[103] So, you experience a supernatural presence of these attributes as you shine with Him out of you. You

---

98 Revelation 21:21

99 Strong's Concordance Hebrew 3303

100 Matthew 5:14

101 Malachi 3:16-17

102 Genesis 1:3

103 Romans 14:17

can't get here by works, but by a relationship you have formed with experiencing Him.

Let's remember where we have been in our journey. First and foremost, God wants you to become His precious treasure. He wants you to get rid of what is dead in your life, and that is anything that separates you from God and leave what is dead behind. You have been tried and tested in the fire and now you have the right to walk on streets paved in gold.[104] You are the temple of God and He resides in more and more of you. You get rid of the things that adorn you and replace them with the jewels of the kingdom, and you become beautiful. As you get more of God, and you get more by hearing the Word of God and allowing His Holy Spirit to come into you, then, you can enter heaven through the gates of pearl.

As you reach deeper and deeper with the Holy Spirit, the anointing will teach you all things,[105] you can now become a disciple of God. You become able to do this by wanting to become all God wants you to be, and asking for all of what God has got for you. Then, under the relationship you develop with enjoying Him and His discipline – you follow His process for transformation which is the ability to let Him show you what you need to take off, and the obedience to take it off and you moved up into discipleship.

Welcome, O disciple of the Lord. Welcome into the inner courts of the Lord, where He shows you mysteries you have only dreamt you would experience. Let your light so shine before men, that they may see your good works, and glorify your Father who is in heaven![106]

This next Scripture sums up what this process truly is.

---

[104] Revelation 21:21

[105] 1 John 2:27

[106] Matthew 5:16

Now the Lord is that Spirit: and where the Spirit of the Lord is, there is liberty. But we all, with open face beholding as in a glass the glory of the Lord, are changed into the same image from glory to glory, even as by the Spirit of the Lord.[107]

The process is where we travel from glory to glory in our experiencing more of what God has inside His limitless kingdom for us. We behold as in a glass, like a mirror, the light that God puts inside of us. The Holy Spirit brings us the liberty from what trapped us before, the false beliefs we held, the sin God wants us to get released from. We are released from the false into the liberty, the freedom that Jesus wants to bring to us. He puts His freedom inside of us. As we are doing this, we can only see a bit of how much glory there is. We see into a piece of heaven that we are allowed to see and we are changed into the same image, the same creation as Christ. We continue to do this again and again, as the Spirit of the Lord continues to change us into God's image. Isn't this amazing? Through our brokenness, our mess ups, our false way of thinking, as we give God permission, it comes right out and in those places more of Him comes in. This is how He disciples us because we are His treasure.

---

[107] 2 Corinthians 3:17-18

TREASURE

CHAPTER SIX

BRIDES and FEASTS, PARTIES and BAR MITZVAS

There is fun to be had!

Becoming the bride – what is God really looking for?

God is about celebrating and about forming covenants.

WE MUST HAVE FUN and BE IN COVENANT

Now that you've entered into heaven, a true disciple of Christ, you are seated at the Feast! There's a wedding coming – the biggest wedding of all time. Our King is coming and He's looking for a Bride. Beauty, remember it is the light in us, is adorned like a bride. Jesus, who is the Bridegroom comes and sweeps us off our feet. He literally comes in and pours Himself forth as a husband waiting to meet us at the altar. God wants to take our hands and make an everlasting covenant. Will we allow Him to come into the secret and private inner chamber of our heart and reach all of those places we are afraid to reveal?

What should we do to become the bride? First and foremost we must accept the covenant that God offers us. The meaning of a covenant is that it is a solemn and binding agreement made.[108] This agreement is one that is seriously and thoughtfully made and not to be taken lightly.

A solemn agreement is done alone. No one can do this for you. Crossing the altar into a deeper agreement with God means there will be no turning back. Coming into the marriage with God is serious business. Jesus placed His life

---

[108] Webster's Dictionary

into the hands of Papa God and did whatever was required to bind this agreement He had.

It was prophesied to me that there was to be no turning back. For several years I had this little back door that would open where I would want to go back, but the Lord spoke this Word to me, and then, it was confirmed by another prophet. There was no turning back. I was now entering the place of no return to my old life, but into the one I had been asking for. What God had for me was a one-way trip and I had asked Him to make me a His disciple. I wanted to fulfill all God had for me in this life. My journey has come with many trials and much testing. There truly is no turning back. We must remember Jesus when He said, No man having put his hand to the plow, and looking back, is fit for the kingdom of God.[109] When we are treasure, we have to learn how to act and be treasure. Real treasure is pure. It is valued and properly taken care of. It stands for those to remark about its beauty, its light, its value to the one who possesses it. If God possesses us, and we have surrendered our lives to Him, then, we must press in. To press in means to spend the time with God to receive more of Him. We go in for answers to our situations but God answers back with more of Him, and then, we receive more and trust Him with our situations.

I can tell you first hand this can be hard, but oh, is it worth it! Let's see where we aren't surrendered to God and place ourselves at His mercy – and at the feet of Jesus do we enter into a deeper walk with Him. The more we bend to the will of our Maker, the more He pours in riches and glory into our lives. Jesus knew there was so much to the kingdom that it was ridiculous to look back. To accept the counterfeit after you have tasted the real is not fit for those who are called by God to be His possession. That is why He says not to look

---

[109] Luke 9:62

back. Jesus knew we needed to remember these things and to yearn for more of Him.

As we desire deeper fellowship, deeper love, deeper relationship, and more of heaven coming down in us, we must for once and for all leave behind what was and will never be again. This is the true marriage. You commit to go through together no matter what. There are mountains to stand on top of and there are valleys to cross.

I speak from experience in my own marriage. John and I have been married for more than twenty years. He and I are night and day in many respects. He has a different kind of calling than I do and it makes us go in opposite directions a lot of the time. Yet, I have to lay down my will for God's perfect will and so does John. Do we love each other? Yes, we do. Yet, because John is called out to the secular music world, to find that one lost sheep that the Lord wants to touch, and I am called into the inner courts with the Lord and to prophesy and minister in the church, it can make our directions feel opposing. Yet, we are both committed to carry out what God has for us even if we are going in different directions on the earth and in the body of Christ.

Long term, committed relationships do what is necessary for the betterment of the relationship. The relationship becomes the most important element between two people. We must serve the Lord and put ourselves in the picture, but recognize that what God asks of us may not always be the easiest way. God's way is the best way for the relationship. It is the higher way. The relationship becomes a Person between the two separate people. Each person must be sensitive to the relationship in order for it to succeed. This is similar to the way we are to be sensitive to the presence of the Holy Spirit in order to receive more of God. If we respect and honor this relationship, the marriage covenant grows strong. It is the same way with our relationship with God.

Sometimes we go through valleys or difficulties in our walk but between these low points there is much joy. There is much celebrating. God's drenching, supernatural, wonderful love pours inside of you and you must open up to experience and see things that you didn't know were ever possible. God sets up a feast for you right in front of your enemies.[110] He celebrates you. He dances with you. He sings to you and takes you into the deep recesses of His heart. He shares with you His tenderness. He fills up your heart because He's taken out your heart of stone and replaced it with a heart of flesh.[111] The root meaning of flesh means to be fresh, full, to announce, preach, and tell good things.[112] This is true success!

This love affair opens with a tender, innocent, pure bride who waits for His every touch and move that He makes over her life. The bride waits in expectation and breathlessness of what He will do next. When He leaves she winces, she mourns, she awaits the return of Him and cries out for His Presence. When He arrives she hushes, she gasps, she holds her breath at what the God of all creation may be planning. Our God is full of surprises and He loves to surprise you with big things and little things, things that only He could know about you. You are that bride.

He draws you to worship Him because you discover more and more of Him – and He assures you this is just the beginning! This is just the first night of an everlasting journey with Him leading and you following, with Him carving trails and you uncovering the adventure.

Remember the five things we needed in our treasure hunting? They are: 1) the risk of death; 2) leaving behind comfort of what was normal and safe; 3) not

---

[110] Psalms 23:5

[111] Ezekiel 11:19

[112] Strong's Concordance Hebrew 1320, root word 1319

doing things by a religious 'legalistic' rule system; 4) the promise of adventure; 5) the promise of amazing riches.

We have entered into all five places when we have reached this place in our journey as the bride of Christ. We risk our lives to follow this because the world does not recognize our King and wants to destroy Him. We leave behind comfort to do whatever our Lord asks of us. (If we are concerned about the Word we receive from the Holy Spirit, we test it[113] and get it confirmed by the mouth of two or three witnesses.[114]) We don't follow the world's laws, we follow our God who leads us in higher ways. We experience adventure as we step out and He shows up with signs and wonders following. He shows us big and small things that confirm He is right there walking with us. We become vessels of light that hold amazing riches that He pours inside of us and we receive such joy as we take hold of this work. We are reaching the place of true fulfillment in our calling.

Then, God does something even greater. He brings the kingdom down to us in larger doses. The bride is God's city, His kingdom coming down to earth for us to covenant with.[115] This is the part of the journey we have been born for. This is the time in the history of the Bride that we are getting to be part of. John saw it in Revelation and we are getting to experience it as believers across the nations. Read what John said. "And I John saw the holy city, new Jerusalem, coming down from God out of heaven, prepared as a bride adorned for her husband."[116]

His kingdom, which drops down from heaven right on top of earth, right in the middle of us and our stuff, is what we were made to experience. The earth is God's footstool.[117] He rests His feet upon us as the earth. Since we learn in

---

[113] 1 John 4:1

[114] Matthew 18:16

[115] Revelation 21:9

[116] Revelation 21:2

Scripture that we put peace on as our shoes,[118] we can then reason that the peace that Jesus gives to us, not as the world gives to us but as God gives to us, is what is coming down. Heaven lands in our midst. God wants to come down and celebrate with us just how good He is. And what do we do?

We worship God of course!

We celebrate and enjoy His presence and all that He is.

If this isn't happening to you, if this isn't happening in your church, then ask God to bring it! Ask God to make it happen. If you are not passionate about God, ask the Lord to show you so that you can have all you were created to have as a child of God! God is long-suffering and patient with us, but we all have a fixed time to be here on earth to do what we were created to do. Each day is important. Each day should not be wasted. Ask for more of Him so that you can get passionate about Him. He may move you or move heaven toward you, but He rewards those that diligently seek Him.[119] He loves it when we're crazy about Him. He loves it when we can't get enough of Him.

He loves parties – He created them. He loves food and drink[120] (remember, He's got a new wine for us that doesn't look like the one in the natural). He loves laughter, dancing and celebration. God wants us free to celebrate. David, who can be read about in 1 and 2 Samuel, had God's heart because he had entered into God's love as a boy and never left God's love. Love is the core of God. David knew this love. He followed and held to it, even when he sinned and set up a murder so he could have another man's wife. When David was faced with his own sin what did he do? He ran right to God.[121] We must turn

---

[117] Acts 7:48-49

[118] Ephesians 6:15

[119] Hebrews 11:6

[120] Luke 5:36-39, Acts 2:15-21

[121] 2 Samuel 12:13

toward love and not away. We must allow love to draw us and let us "dance wildly in the streets" as my first pastor would say.

God wants us to celebrate life, love, happiness and all that He's given us. Yes, there is time to be serious but we have made the covenant with God and have entered in through the gates of pearl (our former pain now covered by the Lord) and entered heaven. God wants us to enjoy our lives. We are treasure and we are treasured by the Creator of all there is and will ever be.

If you doubt God wants you to celebrate, let's look for a minute at two things.

The first one is about Jesus and His first miracle.[122] He turned water into wine. Where? At a wedding feast. The guests had finished everything and they wanted more. What did God do? God said, sure, you want more. Great. Let's celebrate. Water became wine and what Jesus served was better than the best the world had to offer. When God comes He brings what is better than what the world has.

The second thing is this: Jesus says He brought His kingdom with Him.[123] It doesn't come from earth. It comes from heaven. This, of course, really ticks off the enemy. He doesn't want us to celebrate. He doesn't want us to enjoy heaven dropping on earth. Why? Because Satan was the leader of celebration in heaven and we're not celebrating him. We are celebrating God. The thing that Satan wanted more than anything was to be celebrated and he'll never have it.

Celebration in the world is empty. My husband, John Ford Coley, has spoken about how empty being celebrated in the world is. When he got his first gold record, he was in Toronto, Canada and was 27 years old. He was walking the streets there with his former partner and the news that they had finally achieved what they had worked so hard for came. One million records had been

---

[122] John 2:1-10

[123] Luke 22:29

sold. They were on every radio station across the nation and most of the world. What should have brought great fulfillment brought great emptiness. It was nice and all, but the void was so deep and wide that it haunted John.

This is because the world's high places are not like God's high places. They do not bring wholeness or lasting joy. They are more like addictions. You receive the accolade for a moment, but then you have to get more in order to sustain your self-worth. It becomes a cycle you have to continue to repeat in order to maintain some level of self worth. When you can't find it, you may turn to other addictions: drugs, sex, relationships, food, fame, money, acquiring things. This is because you can't find what you are truly looking for and deep inside, you know there's more and you just can't locate it. Anything that isn't God operates like this. You have to keep consuming because you are empty. That's because it is empty on the outside of God and these things of life were never made to fulfill us.

God's celebration operates in an entirely different way. Only the celebration of what God gives us brings the eruption of absolute greatness inside of us. God designed it that way because He made us to walk with Him in the cool of the day.[124] If God is the center of our celebration then, whatever great things we receive in our outer life come into right balance. We must have what's on the inside in order to enjoy what comes on the outside. My husband John Ford Coley had the outer experience of fame and fortune but was missing the inner experience of God's complete love. He was singing songs like 'Love is the Answer' but he wasn't finding his own inner answers. That inner joy came to him years later when he accepted Jesus Christ.

This is why the Apostle Paul spoke about how he could be content whether he was abounding or abased.[125] He had entered into the inner experience with

---

[124] Genesis 3:8

[125] Philippians 4:12

God – the inner courts of God's presence - where all love flows and so the outer experiences – life's outward circumstances were less important to him.

Do you have this inner peace, this inner joy that God brings down to wrap around you? If you don't, or if you want more of this, let's ask God right now to give it to you. Do you want that inner walk? Are you ready to make the one way commitment to become a disciple? If your answer is yes, then say this prayer out loud:

God, I really want all you have for me.

I know there's no turning back.

I want the secret places,

the Holy Covenant,

and to become your disciple, Jesus.

I ask that You bring heaven down

so that I can celebrate You.

Thank you, Lord.

In Jesus Name, I pray. Amen.

Now that you have made this commitment, be willing to make some life changes that will draw you closer to the King. These are the life changes you made when we looked at what you might have to be willing to lay down in order to have what God wants to give you. Assure yourself that God always gives back more than He ever takes away.

Let's look at these things we might have to give up in order to have the better life God wants to give us in order to be prepared for the shift that is coming.

Will you lay down what you treasure?

- your time?

- your possessions?

- your relationships?

- your power?

- your privacy?

- your success?

- your travel?

- your family?

Jesus did this for us. He obtained the treasure of the whole world for following the treasure map that God led him to follow. He was hunting for treasure and it required the following: 1) the risk of death; 2) His leaving behind comfort of what was normal and safe; 3) His not doing things by a religious 'legalistic' rule system; 4) the promise of adventure; 5) the promise of amazing riches.

Jesus was hunting for treasure and that treasure is you. Remember, you are precious treasure. You are what Jesus died to possess. He offered us that we might have life and have it more abundantly.[126] You are now going to enter more of that abundant life because you have agreed to make the covenant. You have signed on to become a disciple of Christ. You are TREASURE. Let's move now to see what territory you are going to gain.

TREASURE

CHAPTER SEVEN

LAND, TERRITORY, CITIES and REGIONS

Everything belongs to God.

He says He will give nations to us

but we must do what He instructs as our Lord.

How do we treasure what God gives us?

WE MUST LEARN STEWARDSHIP

The earth is quite a treasure! What a planet we live on! Our next step as the Sons and Daughters of the living God is that NOW WE ARE TO TAKE NATIONS! Yes, nations. God will give us nations and places, territories and regions. We will have heavenly rights that supersede all earthly rights as we step into destiny with our Lord God. It gets thick, it gets wide and it gets very, very deep as we enter these kinds of levels with God. This is no longer a milk mindset where we are beginning in our relationship with God. It is a kingdom mindset for a kingdom people. It requires a maturity in our lives.

---

[126] John 10:10

THE KINGDOM

Let's imagine a scene in our minds to grasp what God is trying to give to us. Let's move back to the days of Kings and Queens, horses, swords and mighty battles. This is the place of the kingdom and the place for us to move into. Picture your King. He is tall and has a long face, but all wisdom resides in His veins. He is equipped to call a legion of soldiers behind Him at any time. He looks across His endless and vast empire, but calls YOU into His inner court.

Of course, you don't feel qualified or even know why you have been chosen. You begin to remember all your shortcomings and all your mistakes. The King knows what you've been thinking and says for you to look at Him, look at His empire, His army, His vast resources. You aren't to rely on your own power but you are to rely on His power. He will be at your side. He will lead you into battle. He will show you the plans of the enemy.

You begin to feel a little more confident. You say to yourself, I can't go wrong. The King is going with me. I'm not in charge. He's in charge. As you begin to change the way you are thinking to the way the King wants you to think, He begins to smile and folds His arms watching your transformation. He is happy that you are now seeing things His way. He places on your head a crown. He puts a robe around your shoulders. He puts a ring, with His signature on it on your finger. Others that see you can see a shift in you, a change of position, and you begin to gain in the confidence because of your new position inside the security of your King.

This is the position that you have as a Son and a Daughter of God. He is ready to hand you nations, kingdoms, inheritances, land, position, placement, wealth, riches, glory, and power. You must seize it. You must stand in it. He will have one person take government because the government rests upon His shoulders.[127] He will have another take Wall Street because all the earth is His.[128]

---

[127] Isaiah 9:6

He will put one in a school, another in a court, another in the mall, and another in the Church. He needs us to take places, cities, land, homes, and neighborhoods. Each part and piece is important to God. All jobs are important. There is never one too small or one too large. They all fit together in His design to prepare the earth for His arrival.

Jesus, our King, has many ready to do His work and if you won't take your place, He will give it to another.[129] Yet, He has been working on this project since the beginning. He has had this plan, this grand design of what He wanted to accomplish in order to complete the dream He has. God wanted to make a people that would love Him because they knew Him, they discovered Him, whether it be in a church or in a science experiment. God made us with free will, with the freedom to choose Him and you have chosen Him, and He is pleased.

You are sincerely His treasure. You have committed yourself to follow Him and honor Him. He commits to give you a heart to know Him, and be His people, and He will be your God.[130]

As God's treasure, we're not to organize ourselves the way the world would want us to – as adorning ourselves with what is valued by mankind. We're to stand meekly and allow God to bless us with our inheritance – regions, lands, nations and the globe.

---

[128] Psalms 24:1

[129] Matthew 25:28-29

[130] Jeremiah 24:7

God doesn't want us to borrow because we already have full and complete ownership. That is the key to faith. We must recognize what we have in heaven and pull it down to earth. The meaning of treasure in the Strong's Concordance is a depository, storehouse, or treasure house. God doesn't want us to receive anything but what He has to give us. He will unfold his treasures before us but

> The Lord shall open unto this His good treasure,
>
> the heaven to give rain unto thy land in His season,
>
> and to bless all the work of thine hand:
>
> and thou shall lend unto many nations,
>
> and thou shalt not borrow.
>
> Deuteronomy 28:12

we have to learn how to take care of what we have.

God says to us to be faithful in little and He will make us a ruler over much.[131] This is a simple principle and no matter where we are, this is what we must do to the best of our ability. God will not give us more than we can handle and He wants to give us much, but we must take care of what we have, be responsible with it and not extreme with it, not losing our peace about it. We must accept the little we are to be faithful with, not decide that it's not good enough. Of course, we are going to make mistakes along the way but they aren't mistakes if we don't repeat them. They are lessons. They are mistakes if we continue to make them and do not receive the lesson God is trying to give us. Our God is long suffering and ever patient with us, but He wants us to succeed and we want to succeed so we can receive all He wants to give us! This could be called a Win-Win situation. We sign up, He changes us, He leads us, and we win.

Okay, so here's a funny story about how God has made me. One of the first jobs I had in the church was to volunteer to do some office work one day a week. When I arrived, the pastor asked me if I would mind cleaning up the bathrooms and a hallway. The janitor was absent that week and couldn't make it. Sure. I gladly accepted. I was so on fire with God inside me that I felt so privileged to clean His house. I mean, the Maker of heaven and earth had come down and was dwelling inside me. I got to come to church – a place that filled up with His Presence. God actually came inside this place I was in – so cleaning up His place was a thrill. It was a one-time request and then I served making copies of audio tapes of sermons.

My serving continued. Next, I volunteered with the babies. My daughter was little and I brought her along to help. After that, God moved us into another church. My husband and I helped with junior high kids, teaching them one Sunday a month. After that, we moved to our current church. There, we did Wednesday night dinner preparations for a few years. My husband also

---

[131] Matthew 25:21

helped park cars and take tithes and offerings as an usher. The Lord then moved me into Prophetic ministry where I served on a team and then, onto the ministry team for the church. I continued to be faithful and He moved me up to help more and more in ministry. Now, I was freely prophesying in my church, as the Lord led me as well as got moved up to Team Captain at prophetic activations in the Prophetic ministry call.

This was all part of God's plan. I tell you this to make a point – not to point out places that I have been to. I was in charge of Disney's creative management for Disneyland Paris when it was being built. Yet, God had me cleaning bathrooms. Humble yourself before the Lord – all jobs are important before God. They may not be before man, but they are before God. My brother who is in ministry told me a story about arriving at a conference extra early when he was a new believer. He thought he was doing such a great job by getting their extra early. It would show God how much he wanted what God had. When he went into the sanctuary he saw a man vacuuming the rugs. The man got there at 5 a.m., an hour before my brother arrived. This man was the speaker. This was the leader of a large church denomination who was leading by example. He wasn't doing it from a place of 'must' or 'had to' he just loved God and wanted to share what he had with others. He had a spirit of excellence inside of Him.

A key to going up with God is that when there's a job God shows you, no matter how small, go ahead and do it as the Lord leads. Don't do it from a place of fear because fear is not God, but do it from a place of love because God is love. When we love, we reach out and take care. We are owners, not renters, and we serve from a place of joy.

Now, the funny part of the story is that whenever I go into the church's restroom and I see paper on the floor, I have to clean it up. I don't have God's holy unction encouraging me to do it. It's just that this is my Papa's house. This is where His presence comes into the building and resides within us. The point isn't about me and what I've been doing in church. The point is that you can see the progression where God moves one step at a time, one place at a time. He sees what we are willing to do and if we can do this job, He will bring us into another one. Be faithful in little. Toilet paper on the floor is little but my Father's House is where I receive so much. I want to take care of it.

God tests us with a little and as we learn to handle what He's given us to be in charge of, He'll add more. If we fail to handle it, He'll give it to another.[132] God tests us with money, possessions, children, and our relationship with other believers. Everything we have and everywhere we are is a test. Call it a quiz if it makes you feel better. God's not mad at you. Don't feel like He's looking over your shoulder. Realize He wants to give you more. He wants to give you all sorts of things He's got stored up in heaven. He just uses these things to promote us. He looks at our heart. If you are faithful in the little things, God will make you a ruler over much.[133]

God wants to take us and make us overseers of the earth. We are to be stewards over our personal bodies, our families, our cities, our states, our countries and anything that belongs to our Lord. You see, God wants to give it to us. He really does. He is searching the earth to see who has a perfect heart toward Him[134]. It does not say who *is* perfect. It says who has a perfect heart toward Him. When you fall short, run to Him. He wants to show His strength in your life. His strength is made perfect in our weakness[135]. So, we mess up. We run to Him. He picks us up. He teaches us some things. He pours more of Himself inside of us, and we continue like this as we are perfected into His likeness.

---

[132] Luke 16:1-13

[133] Matthew 25:24

[134] 2 Chronicles 16:9

[135] 2 Corinthians 12:9

> **Webster's Dictionary Definition**
>
> steward:
>
> A person appointed to manage the domestic and business affairs of a large household or estate.

We'll never get there. If we did, we wouldn't need Him. What happen, though, is that we become dependent on Him. We become complete with Him and incomplete without Him. We enter into who He is and soar in our relationship with Him. We enter into experiencing God and He enters into us. We learn and grow, and now we make good stewards. There's enough of Him in us to do the job the way it should be done.

There are two examples of bad stewardship I'm going to discuss. God allows us to fall on our knees a lot as we struggle along. We must be faithful with what God has us assigned to now. We all fall short of this. I know I do. There are certain assignments that I have that I don't enjoy doing. I have no gifting in these areas. Yet, from time to time, the Lord will address this and I will do the work I don't want to do. One is my cat box. It's a job that I know I should do, but I don't enjoy it. It's now falling to my son, and he gets a payment for cleaning it out. I see him procrastinate just the way I have done. My bad stewardship in this area is falling right on top of him. Ouch.

Another area is that there was a time when I just ignored our house. I hated the indoor-outdoor carpet in the kitchen and dining room. It was a bleak color of gray and so hard for me to look at. I ignored sweeping the floors. My kids were little and so there were many crumbs that lived on the floor. One day, I was watching TV and the Spirit of the Lord came, spoke some revelation to my heart, and bam! down onto the floor I went. When you fall out with God like that, there's no pain. So, I remained on the floor, laughing at what the Spirit of God had just done. Then, I looked over and there, next to me was a really crumby floor.

The Holy Spirit spoke and said, "Now you know why you need to clean the floor."

I laughed ever more from God's joke. He is a kind teacher. He was right. I wasn't doing my job. He lovingly pointed it out as he was giving me so much of Him at the same time. (By the way, I now sweep much more often and we have the most beautiful tile that John put in with his own hands). I am so glad that God hasn't had me fall into the cat box! Now, that would be quite a mess!

We will get back to accessing more of what God wants to give us. If we are going to gain territory as the treasure of God, if we are going to inhabit what God has for us we must change our thinking and take hard and serious looks at ourselves. We must be trustworthy. We must be responsible if we want a lot from God. We can't be perfect, but we are to move from renters to owners. We must own what we do and who we are in the Lord.

What is it to be trustworthy? Statements like, "It's not my job" "Oh, we're just too busy to help at the church" or "I don't' think I'd be any good at that" are not statements of ownership. Now, if you have serious commitments or know in your spirit that God has you elsewhere, please know that I'm not trying to convict you. I am trying to allow you to look at who you are in the body of Christ. Statements of not getting out of our comfort zone are not good for our growth. They are statements a child makes. A child cannot own property and be responsible for it. It is the duty of an adult. God wants to give us much treasure, but how can He if we won't be mature with our lives? Let's not give Satan any more opportunity to have our stuff. Let's look at what is difficult and get what God has for us. Let's also be led by the Spirit to get involved. Let's not do so much stuff that we lose our joy or balance in our lives. Balance is critical.

The great part is that today is a new day. God's mercies are new every morning. You can change what you've been doing and get into what God is doing right now. This minute. All you have to do is begin with a commitment to do what is right before God.

Let's say this prayer to get on track:

> God,
>
> I want all the treasure you have for me in heaven to come down to earth.
>
> Show me the areas I need to work on Lord so I can have all the treasure you have for me.
>
> Help me become a good steward, Lord.
>
> In Jesus Name I pray.
>
> Amen

Let'
s now discuss the part of stewardship that is about doing things by the rules as our Lord guides us. Since man in and of himself has a sin nature, anything with too much of man will eventually twist and get so bound up there is no breathing room. Jesus did not come to have us go into bondage. He came to set us free! We are to follow the Holy Spirit's leading, always judging what we hear and

measuring it against God's Word. God is not about contradicting Himself. He is not the author of confusion.[136] Yet, as believers who follow God many times we become confused. What we must do is learn how to follow the Spirit's leading and develop our love walk. Each one of us has junk. We have areas of weakness in ourselves and we must come to Christ with all of those areas so that God can fill us up with Him. As we fill up with Him, we mature and grow. The area of our weakness becomes the area of our strength.[137] Jesus, in the Sermon on the Mount, goes into all of these things that each one of these areas of weakness will bring to us if we follow God.[138] There will be times as believers that we must follow as the Lord instructs us, and not another.

Let me give you an example in my own life. When I came into our church, I went to visit the pastor looking for counsel and confessed some areas of weakness in my life. I just wasn't fitting with the women at the church. He asked if I had friends in the church and I told him I had many friends but not many in our church. The pastor said that I needed to find friends in our church and I felt a pressure that I should have my friends there. When I left, I felt great angst about the meeting. The following day, the Lord showed me that ever since I was a kid, I always went from group to group. I never fit into one group of people. In fact, I became antsy when I stayed for too long with one group of people. I felt best when I had friends in different groups rather than in one place. The pastor, being a leader over a flock of sheep, had good advice. However, for the gifting God gave me and the assignment, of being able to speak and reach different groups of people, I was built to go from place to place and not reside with just one group of believers. In this situation, I needed to listen to what God was showing me rather than rely completely on this pastor's well-intentioned advice. I now have many friends in our church as well as

---

[136] 1 Corinthians 14:33

[137] 2 Corinthians 12:9

[138] Matthew 5

friends in many other places. I just had to learn how to balance the counsel I was receiving with the leading of the Lord for my life.

I make the point that there are times when you have to follow God over man. Each time that the Gospel moved forward in great leaps and bounds, this requirement to do what God was telling the believer over what man was instructing, occurred. Martin Luther did it. John Wesley did it. Oral Roberts did it. Paul and Jan Crouch, the founders of Trinity Broadcast Network did it. The Jesus movement that swept through California in the 1970s did it. We must be willing to risk not looking good before men in order to do what God is instructing us to do. We must be true to the unction inside of us because God has a plan for our lives that is special. In order to be special treasure, we must risk looking different. With treasure, it makes us stand out. We need to stand out and stand up in the ways the Holy Spirit is leading us. We can't do this out of rebellion, but we can do this in a Spirit of love and being true to ourselves.

Good stewards learn how to master this with the groups they are with. There are times when you have to be willing to turn over the tables[139] and other times come under the authority of the direction you are given in leadership. Where no counsel is, the people fall.[140] Pray and ask God for the right balance because a false balance is an abomination to the Lord.[141]

Now that you are fully stepping into your stewardship, let's direct you into treasure hunting.

We have now crossed into all the areas of treasure hunting: 1) the risk of death; 2) leaving behind comfort of what was normal and safe; 3) not doing things by a religious 'legalistic' rule system; 4) the promise of adventure; 5) the promise of amazing riches.

---

[139] Matthew 21:12

[140] Proverbs 11:4

[141] Proverbs 11:1

Let's take adventure up a notch and see what God does next. Remember that good stewards receive authority and authority brings down the kingdom and puts it into its rightful place in the earth. You will know when you have reached this level because God will begin to place more and more authority into your hands. It comes to you - you don't chase it. Chase God and the gifts and callings will chase you.[142]

So, if you want this, be faithful in the things He has given you and He will increase what He gives you. He assures us that the people who know Him will be strong and do exploits.[143] We are now inside of discipleship and in the place of knowing Him. God's people are His portion, His treasure, His enjoyment and He loves for us to know Him completely.

This is why we are now up to adventure. God yearns to be on this adventure with you. You have tasted some of His ways, but now let's ask for more. Please read and then, say this prayer:

> God,
>
> I want more adventure.
>
> I want more excitement in the kingdom.
>
> I want to enjoy what You have given me.
>
> Thank you, Lord for sending more to me now.
>
> In Jesus Name, Amen.

This will take us to our next chapter. We are going to be treasure hunters.

---

[142] Luke 12:31

[143] Daniel 11:32

TREASURE

CHAPTER EIGHT

OCEANS, SAILORS, PIRATES and DEEP SEA DIVING

The mysteries and adventures are available

to those who know Him.

WE MUST BE TREASURE HUNTERS

This morning the Lord sent me a dream. I receive them most every morning and then, when I spend time with Him, He reveals the interpretation to me. It has been like this for more than two years. In the dream, I went into a house. It was empty and big, and brand new. It was a mansion with seven rooms in it. We were looking at it and deciding if we wanted to purchase it. I liked how open and vast it felt, how spacious and how high the ceilings were. I loved the big picture windows. It felt really, really good to me in this new mansion.

Then, I was in another house. This one was even larger. It had many, many rooms. There were 28 bedrooms in this house. It was owned by a man who wasn't at the house, but he was returning. There was so much stuff in this house that it was packed, completely full. Each room I entered had more than the room before. It was well decorated, and had lots of different color palettes for each room. It was pretty amazing. There was a woman that came into the room where I was standing. She told me she had decorated the house. I could have this house with all the furnishings for 2.2 million dollars. I went through more and more rooms. There were sofas, shelves, things piled up everywhere. It felt old and historic. It felt like they had collected things and never got rid of anything. It had great value and history to what had happened there. It seemed to go on forever. I went into room after room after room, and more and more things of interest were piled up in each room. Then, my husband joined me. We were considering this house. The woman really wanted us to have it. Somehow, we began following some others and they seemed to get lost in this house. They took us down back ways and roads and it seemed like a dead end journey, all inside this amazingly large and endless mansion.

I finally looked at my husband and suggested we turn around and go in our own direction. That's what we did. We turned and went back out and found our way toward the first room we had entered into. There was the woman. She said the man that was the owner had returned. There was much respect for him but I just wanted to leave. This wasn't a house I wanted and I didn't care how big it was. It had too much history, too much of its own furnishings for me to feel free inside of. I wanted the first house. It was new and beautiful and not too large. It was also a mansion but there was so much I could do with it.

Then, the Lord showed me this is where we are in the journey of this book. You can choose the new house that Jesus wants to give you. It has six bedrooms and one room to just sit and rest in. Seven is the number that God uses for things to be completed. God created in six days and rested on the seventh. In the seventh bedroom of your new house, you can rest and get what you need to enjoy creating the other six rooms He has given you.

The new house God wants to give you is free of charge to you, who take Jesus Christ at his Word.

> Let not your heart be troubled:
> Ye believe in God, believe also in Me.
> In My Father's house there are many mansions:
> if it were not so, I would have told you.
> I go to prepare a place for you.
> And if I go to prepare a place for you
> I will come again and receive you unto Myself;
> that where I am, there ye may be also.
> And whither I go ye know, and the way ye know.
> John 14:1-4

I have heard people assume that Jesus is talking about a place in heaven and that's what I thought, too. Then, God sent me this dream. "In My Father's House there are many mansions and I go to prepare a place for you." Not only do we have the opportunity to receive mansions in heaven, but we can receive them right here on earth. Jesus talks about what He's going to prepare for us, so He can bring it to us. Jesus is bringing mansions for us to live in while we are here on earth. The Lord's Prayer also verifies this reality. "Our Father, who art in heaven, hallowed be Thy name, Thy kingdom come. Thy will be done, as in heaven, so in earth."[144]

Jesus is bringing, as part of your treasure, a mansion for you to live in.

His Father, our God, has many mansions.

Don't you want a new mansion to live in?

This is what God has for you as treasure. The ultimate treasure that God wants to give to you is that you are housed within His houses. You are treasured inside of His treasure. You are a King inside of His kingdom. Isn't that amazing? That's what God is talking about. That's what the kingdom is for.

The mansion on earth that Jesus wants to give you is new. It's the heavenly places you live in when God gives you His kingdom. The Word describes this when we are told that we sit in heavenly places in Christ Jesus.[145] We are built up together for a habitation of God through the Spirit.[146] Habitation in the Webster's dictionary is a dwelling place, a residence. This is one of the definitions about the mansion Jesus has said He's going to go build for us to live in.

Now, let's talk about the second house that was offered in my dream. It comes with a price. It comes at the price of your freedom, for you will have to work very hard to get this house, and the owner will always be looming for you to make payments that you seem unable to make. It comes with pressure, and worry, and wants, and has a lot of your history and piles of your junk. This house holds onto you like ropes that tie you down when you know you should soar. This is the house that Adam stepped into when he left the mansion and the kingdom God had built him. The enemy is the lord over this house.

---

[144] Luke 11:2

[145] Ephesians 2:6

[146] Ephesians 2:22

The new house is set up the way the Lord will arrange things. He knows just where to place all the items and to arrange all the activities. He allows us to select the paint, colors and styles because He put it inside of us to like and desire these things. It's fun and free, and a joy to be in because Jesus has built this place just for you.

The other house is the way man in his own flesh lives. It becomes heavy with all of the pain, burdens, memories and regrets of our lives.

The new seven-room house has high ceilings and you can place new furnishings, new things you will sit on and rest in. There's not much in it, because it is always new. Every day in your new house you get new things. Every day in your new house you have new revelation and new peace, and a new freedom that washes over you.

You are always free to go back to your old house. You can go back to generations of your junk, your family history, and generations of doing it a certain way. You can live in endless rooms of clutter, familiarity, and more stuff than you could ever make your way through.

It's your choice. Will you take the step to do the new? Will you accept the new house Jesus wants to put you inside of? Or will you go back to the endless old house that has 28 rooms.

He showed me that the number two stands for covenant and eight is the number of new beginnings. When we add eight and two together, we get the sum of the number ten, which is order. It's the the number of multiplication. Your old house, as you stay in it, multiplies your shortcomings, your pain, your anger, your memories, and your grief. You can stay in that place and you can have order or a better word, control. You will on some level feel you are controlling your life. Your life will be good and you will do things for the Lord and you will be saved, and you will be a believer and live in the house which generations of believers before you have lived in. Yet, something that is not God will reside in that house with you.

Or, you can go into an entirely new house. You can come under a new experience. You can have your entire life, your entire walk, everything you have dared to dream about move into a higher level when you trust Jesus Christ to take the steps needed to enter into this new house Jesus Christ wants to give you. You can have completion of God's plan in your life or you can have your own order, living under the rule of another owner who wants to sell you down the river at a big cost to you, but you can't have both. You can sleep in a different room for almost a month in your old house, running from room to room to try and avoid what you need to face. Or you can bring your old house to Jesus, and become the treasure you were designed to be. I don't know about you, but for me, I am surrendering to whatever the Holy Spirit shows me and receiving that mansion Jesus died to give me.

As I take this new mansion, I enter into the area of adventure with God. This is the abundant life Jesus says you might have. This is where Jesus makes all things new. This is the place where Peter stepped out of the boat and walked on water because He believed if Jesus could do it, so could He. Which house will you live in - the one with all the rooms that is familiar? Or the new one that Jesus wants to give to you? It's all up to you.

Many are called. Few are chosen.[147]

I choose the new house.

It is complete. It has so much possibility. It is fresh. All of my senses receive the new thing God wants to do with me. This is the meaning of God taking out a heart of stone and giving us a new heart of flesh. He says He'll put a new Spirit within us.[148] This will happen if we choose to let go of our old life and receive the new house God has for us to live in.

---

[147] Matthew 22:14

Do you want it?

Do you crave to live in a house that is free from worry and guilt and shame?

Do you want to live in a place where you have each day as a new day, a new adventure where you have no worries and fear cannot reach you?

It's possible. The impossible thing that you have been craving is possible with God. This is what Jesus wants to give you.

Will you take it?

You see, you have to take it by faith.

Without faith, it's impossible to please God. He wants you to receive your mansion by faith.

Just say it.

I will take my mansion by faith, Lord.

That's all you need to say.

If you are truly a disciple of Christ, if this is the commitment in your heart, then there really is no choice. Once you have made this choice, there is no turning back. Nothing is holding you bound or back. You want what your King has for you, new, every day. You are truly a treasure hunter. You are ready to fill up your new house with the new treasures God is going to reveal to you.

So, this brings us to the end of our journey.

Which house you are going to live in? Well, it's up to you. You can choose to have the easier path and stay with all of your stuff, your history, your possessions, your things. You see, God has made you rich in so many ways already. So, here you stand. Yes, here you stand at the threshold of more. You

---

[148] Ezekiel 11:19

stand recognizing that you are treasure. God has completely prepared you for this choice, this amazing choice He gives to you.

What will you choose?

This is entirely up to you. Here, you must count the cost.

Remember, we have promised you the following things: 1) the risk of death; 2) leaving behind comfort of what was normal and safe; 3) not doing things by a religious 'legalistic' rule system; 4) the promise of adventure; 5) the promise of amazing riches. These are the things that are ahead for you in the new house, the new mansion Jesus wants to give you.

Jesus asks you now, which one will you choose?

Will you choose to stay in your old house, which has many of your things in it? Or will you choose to go into the new house God wants to give you?

No one can make this choice for you. It's all up to you.

Again, the kingdom of heaven is like treasure hidden in a field; which a man found and hid; and for joy over it he goes and sells all that he has, and buys that field.[149]

God bless you, my friend.

#

---

[149] Matthew 13:44 NKJV